Instructor's Manual

the Production Game™

Instructor's Manual

the
Production
Game™

D. Keith Denton

Southwest Missouri State University

Addison-Wesley Publishing Company
Reading, Massachusetts • Menlo Park, California • New York
Don Mills, Ontario • Wokingham, England • Amsterdam • Bonn
Sydney • Singapore • Tokyo • Madrid • San Juan

ISBN 0-201-51668-3
ABCDEFGHIJ–BK–943210

PREFACE

The Production Game™simulates the real world production environment. It is not a computer based game, nor is it a board game. Instead it involves human interaction where participants form their own company, produce a product and services and then reassess and improve their performance--all in a classroom setting. Students are actively involved in learning rather than passively listening to a lecture. The game also gives the lecturer a new medium for encouraging learning.

This unique simulation is highly flexible. It can be used in university teaching or corporate training programs. The degree of difficulty of the simulation ranges from a <u>basic option</u> that is meant to be used as a supplement to courses to more <u>advanced options</u> that arc so complete it can be used as a stand-alone course.

The simulation has been used in introductory Production/Operation Management (P/OM) courses that are taught in business schools. It has also been used in manufacturing courses offered through engineering and technology courses. It can be used as a supplement to introductory management courses or be a key feature of advanced production and graduate courses. It also provides an excellent vehicle for many corporate training activities and non-credit managerial training. As you will see it is fun to run, easy to use, and a rewarding experience for both the instructor and participants.

IT'S FUN

It is fun because it provides a powerful learning tool by giving students a feel for what they really have to do to succeed in business--satisfy the customer. Many students and most adults are sick of lectures. That is about all they have had since first grade. The Production Game™provides an exciting alternative where students learn by doing, not by passively sitting in a class.

The first time you run this experiential activity, I think you will be shocked at how little students are able to transfer lecture material to real-life situations. They often fail to do the simplest things, like train their people. It is often amazing to find managers in the simulation doing the wrong things, like doing the employee's job and not theirs. I am sure they know they should be planning, organizing, controlling, directing and so forth, but they frequently do not remember it in a real-life situation. Perhaps it is too many years of passively listening, watching films and memorizing materials for tests.

This is a chance to truly challenge them. I know from experience that they do have fun, but most importantly learn from the exercise. You probably will also find, as I did, that your students' evaluations of your teaching abilities will improve the more you use it. It is just a more interactive, dynamic means of communicating management concepts; one which most students appreciate.

IT'S EASY

It is easy. The material has been class tested for several years. In a few short pages, this instructor's manual will show you how to run the simulation, show you what to look for and provide you with everything you will need to present a first-class simulation. The package for the Production Game™ also contains an Instruction and Study Guide for students or other participants in the simulation. The guide shows students how to play the game and how to win (making their product producible and profitable), and it provides them with the necessary production forms to help them analyze and improve their performance. Their manual will tell them all they need to know. As the instructor, all you need to do is to tell them how they will be evaluated (see section four) and what product or products (see section two) they will need to produce.

IT'S REWARDING

It is rewarding to be appreciated. Most students will appreciate the experience and your efforts. Because the game is highly flexible, you can adjust it to suit your needs and your personality. Each teacher will operate it differently, just as each lectures differently; therefore, it will not appear "canned" and will be a more natural part of the learning experience.

From a teacher's perspective, it is also rewarding to see active, engaged minds. You can see students learning from one production run to the next. Students are excited because they can see the relationship between what they are doing and the real world. They are getting hands-on experience, and their abilities are improving because the experience is occurring in a classroom environment where the lecturer can focus their attention on areas that need improving.

LOCAL INVOLVEMENT

A bonus of the simulation is that it provides an effective way of involving the local business community. When I run the simulation, I often ask local CEO's and other practicing managers to come and watch students make a production run. Their insights about the game and business are often remarkable and, in fact, form the basis for the section in the student manual on "How To Win" the game. Examples of these typical "consultants," comments can be seen in section three.

Most practitioners do not like to lecture. The simulation makes it easier to get local managerial involvement because it provides a more informal medium for them to express their knowledge about running an organization. Students are usually very attentive because they just went through a sometimes frustrating, always intense production run and can relate to what the practitioner is saying.

OUTLINE

SECTION I   THE BASICS

HOW IT WORKS

SECTION II   PRODUCT SPECIFICATION SHEETS

SECTION III SUPPLEMENTAL PRODUCTION MATERIALS AND FORMS

SECTION IV FOR TEACHER'S EYES ONLY

Instructor's Manual

the
Production
Game™

SECTION I - THE BASICS

HOW IT WORKS

Additional details about the simulation can be seen in the Student's Instructions Guide. Basically, the instructor is responsible for setting up the rules for the simulation; the participants are the ones who run it. This is the rare case where the more rules the instructor provides, the more the simulation approaches a real life situation. At its most advanced level, instructors may find that they can simply define the parameters of the simulation, and then just step back and watch it materialize. Participants will reorganize themselves when necessary to become more efficient, conduct their own "manager's meetings" and provide a report of the results to the instructor. The instructor, as the customer, simply clarifies what he or she wants from the participant's company.

As already noted in the introduction, this simulation is not a computer-based game. Instead, participants actually run their own company and produce products and provide services within a classroom setting. It can be set up in a job shop arrangement where students make a variety of customer products or as a repetitive operation that provides large amounts of standardized products.

Realism and complexity can vary from the basic option where students are only responsible for managing production, inventory, quality and worker utilization, to more advanced options that involve interaction with suppliers, customers and a full range of business considerations including: finance, investments, employee training and selection, design/manufacturing interaction, purchasing, quality control, maintenance, interpersonal communication and a host of other real life concerns.

In the basic option, students try to simply improve their producibility. In the advanced versions they also must be aware of profitability. It is at this level where the simulation is most realistic because students must be producing quality products and services at maximum efficiency and profitability. In short, producing good stuff at a profit.

The simulation is designed to teach participants, in an interactive hands on manner, how to produce a product and provide related services within a minimum amount of time, while meeting the customer's needs. In order to do this participants must first be allowed to elect their CEO, develop their management team (e.g., design engineers, human resource managers, inventory managers, production managers and so forth), and assign responsibilities and accountabilities.

ORGANIZING IT

Usually one class or a 50 minute period is required for students or trainees to organize their management team. In order for this to go as smoothly as possible, have the students read the first part of their Instructions Guide where it describes "How to Play the Game." This assignment should be given to them before their actual "organizational period" so they can have time to digest the information in the manual. The time the assignment is made would also be a good time for the instructor to tell them what they will be making. Instructors can choose their own product or one of the twenty or so products that are shown in section two of this manual. With initial production runs or when dealing with students with limited managerial skills, it is wise to choose one of the simple products to make.

Once the instructor chooses one of the products, he or she then reviews the product specifications so that students know what will be expected of them. In more advanced versions of the game, students do not know until the day of production exactly what types of products they will make. Sometimes they are given several designs to choose from and they must decide which one is best for them. The reason for this is to analyze the interaction between design and manufacturing, often a critical ingredient to business success. If this ingredient is not important in your version, then simply give them the design ahead of time and focus exclusively on the actual production process.

During this same time, instructors will also want to review with students how they will be evaluated. Several examples of possible grading formats can be seen in section four.

With this initial organization out of the way, future classes can be devoted to making production runs and analyzing what went well and what needs improvement. Once the "company" makes a production run, each management team assesses its own performance then streamlines and improves its organization when needed.

This sequence of making production runs (which usually lasts about 30 minutes) and then assessing their performance can occur as many times as the instructor chooses. In the basic or more simple versions of the game, this analysis occurs immediately after a production run. A practitioner who has been watching a run can be used because the instructor is so busy playing the role of the customer that she or he can overlook some important aspects. If a practitioner observer cannot be found, use a couple of volunteer students per work group and tell them to use the observation sheets provided in section three of their instructions and study guide or ones provided in this manual.

This analysis is critical to making improvements in this production process, so the more analyzers, the better. In later "manager's meetings," participants can review their results and the suggestions of these consultants to come up with improvements they can implement before the next production run. These meetings, depending on the instructor's needs, can occur during the next class period or outside class.

As in industry, there are always improvements that can be made. Each time participants make a production run and analyze the results, they learn something new about producing products and services that satisfy the customer's requirements. The simulation has been used as a supplement to courses and as the only activity students did in an eighteen-week course. They were still making improvements, when the course ended!

The key to making improvements is to insure that participants assess a variety of performance measures such as quality, inventory, labor utilization, profits and so on. Since they collect information on these measures after a run and analyze them during their manager's meetings, they always have areas to improve--just like in industry.

Students are provided a whole series of measures by using the forms and reports that are in section three (Production Forms) of their instructions and study guide. A supplemental form called a Stockholder's Report (given to the instructor) is also provided in section three of this manual. It is used when the instructor wants participants to summarize what happened, what went well, and what changes they intend to make. Requiring a brief report like this from a company's CEO tends to keep their manager's meeting more focused on the problems at hand.

RUNNING THE SIMULATION

In the simulation's simplest form, students are only given one of the product specification and diagram sheets that are seen in section two of this manual. These product specifications are supplied to the students' company by you, their customer. In the simulation, their customer is called The Brokerage House (TBH). The instructor, acting as the CEO of TBH, has the product specification sheets shown in section two of this manual.

As seen, each product specification sheet describes a product like a stop sign or simple T-shaped piece that must be produced in 30 minutes or less. They are also supplied the materials seen in Figure 1. Each company needs a complete set of these materials. Thus, if you have two companies, you need two sets of the material and equipment described in Figure 1.

All of these materials and equipment can be purchased at your local discount store. If you are frugal, it will not break the bank. I purchased eight sets of these materials for $67 from a local discount store. I needed eight sets because I had a large, eight tiered classroom. I made each tier, or row of students, a company. If you have a smaller classroom of four rows of seats, the cost should be less.

While I have always provided students with these basic materials and equipment, in advanced versions of the simulation I always encourage them to purchase whatever technology they think will improve their company's performance (e.g., better glue, templates, pencils, etc.). An exacto knife that can cut multiple layers of construction paper is an obvious improvement in technology over the scissors they are supplied. However, before any new equipment is purchased, I always require students to obtain my approval, so safety is considered. For example, when students want to purchase a sharp object like the

---

STUDENT MANUFACTURING COMPANY

1. <u>Production Equipment</u>
   * 5 scissors
   * 4 rulers
   * 4 pencils
   * 1 bottle of glue stick
2. <u>Raw Materials</u>
   * Scrap paper for students to make practice runs
3. <u>Assessment Tool</u>
   * Square inch measurement table (in students study guide)

THE BROKERAGE HOUSE, INC.

* Twenty sets of product specifications (in Section II of this manual)

* $400,000

MUSCLEMAN CONSTRUCTION COMPANY

* 20 sheets of ten different colored construction paper
* 4 sheets of cardboard (optional)
* Stencil (in Section IV) (optional)
* Tape (optional)
* Markers (optional)
* Stapler (optional)

Figure 1

Material and supplies needed for <u>basic</u> version of The Production Game exacto knife, I will require the operators of the equipment to wear safety protection (glove) so they do not cut themselves.

When you wish to de-emphasize the effects of technology and wish to focus exclusively on the managerial aspects of the game then do not allow any equipment substitutions. Whatever is held constant will focus students' attention on that which varies. If you constantly use the same equipment, students will focus their attention on improving managerial structure, not on technological improvements. When I am teaching students who have limited managerial ability or limited interest in management, I do not allow technology substitutions and instead focus on improving managerial ability to achieve results.

BASIC OPTION

If students have limited skills or they are playing the basic option of the game, then only give them one product specification sheet (of the item they will produce or one similar to it) and the materials and equipment seen in Figure 1 at the time they organize their companies. During their next meeting, and all other future production runs, they will try to make as many of the products as possible. If you are only planning on using one product for all of the production runs then choose one that is fairly complex since students are not as likely to become bored with it. Often this is a good approach when first experimenting with the simulation or when teaching an introductory management course where students have limited management skills.

Sometimes when I run a basic option of the simulation, I have students become accountable for more and more responsibility as their experience and ability improve. For instance, in the students' first production run, they focus exclusively on producing as many acceptable products as possible within the production period.

In the second production run, students must again produce as much as possible, but they also must monitor their raw materials, in work-in-process and finished good inventory. These inventory items are measured in square inches, with a square inch measurement sheet that is included with each student's

Instruction and Study Guide. The companies that are producing the least amount of square inches of excess inventory are the better managed ones.

The ideal goal would be to reduce excess square inches of inventory to zero. This means they used all they had and scheduled the work flow so nothing was left after the production. While this may be a goal in this simulation and in industry, it is doubtful that it will happen, so a realistic objective is to try to make incremental improvements.

The third production run requires students to monitor the first two categories already mentioned, plus their overall quality. Quality, like inventory, is measured in square inches. If a company is creating a large number of square inches of scrap and rework, then design and production can be improved.

A fourth run adds labor utilization considerations to the trio already discussed. A course syllabus in section four of this manual describes one example of students evaluated based on these four criteria. Phasing in criteria in this manner gives the teacher a chance to focus on topical areas and does not overload the student's ability. Some teachers, as I sometimes do, prefer to use all the criteria for each run, thereby insuring a more realistic managerial challenge. Additional criteria like profit, finance, design and human relations criteria can be measured by using various aspects of the advanced option of the stimulation.

ADVANCED OPTION

In more advanced options of the simulation, the process starts out the same with the instructor providing a product specification sheet, but it has a slightly different sequence of events and materials. Those materials can be seen in Figure 2. There are a few changes in what you will need to run the advanced as opposed to the basic option.

The production equipment and raw materials are the same. However, since the advanced version focuses on profits as well as being productive, it is necessary for students to have some start-up cash. Students will use the money to purchase raw materials from their supplier, Muscleman Construction, which is run by the teacher. They will also need the money or checks for managerial salaries and employee pay.

```
┌─────────────────────────────────────────────────────┐
│   STUDENT MANUFACTURING COMPANY                       │
└─────────────────────────────────────────────────────┘
```

1. <u>Production Equipment</u>
   * 5 scissors
   * 4 rulers
   * 4 pencils
   * 1 bottle of glue stick
2. <u>Raw Materials</u>
   * 1 black one half sections of construction paper
   * 2 blue one half sections of construction paper
   * 2 white one half sections of construction paper
3. <u>Financial</u>   4. <u>Assessment Tool</u>
   * $50,000   * square inch measurement table.
                                (in students study guide)

```
┌─────────────────────────────────────────────────────┐
│   THE BROKERAGE HOUSE, INC.                           │
└─────────────────────────────────────────────────────┘
```

* Twenty sets of product specifications (in Section II
  of this manual)

* $400,000

```
┌─────────────────────────────────────────────────────┐
│   MUSCLEMAN CONSTRUCTION COMPANY                      │
└─────────────────────────────────────────────────────┘
```

* 20 sheets of ten different colored construction paper
* 4 sheets of cardboard (optional)
* Stencil (in Section IV) (optional)
* Tape (optional)
* Markers (optional)
* Stapler (optional)

Figure 2

Material and supplies needed for <u>advanced</u> version of The Production Game

Sometimes the teacher may find it beneficial to substitute new production equipment or customer requirements so students will need the cash to purchase items like stencil, tape, markers, templates, better scissors and so forth.

As you probably realized, the students' customer, The Brokerage House, must also have money or checks since they purchase the students' products. Of course, the money is not really necessary to run the game (someone can just keep a tally sheet), but it makes it more fun for both parties. Simulation money that can be used in the game is found at the end of Section four of this manual.

Even in the advanced version, it is probably necessary to do one or two dry runs before full production runs are attempted. It is probably wise at first to give the production team only one simple product (like in the basic option) to attempt to make. After this period, you can give them a choice of designs to choose from. Usually two simple designs and two or three complex ones will be given to the CEO. The company's CEO and, if the students are smart, perhaps their finance and production managers, will review the four or five product specifications submitted to them and decide which items they wish to produce.

The price the customer (instructor) is willing to pay for a finished product ranges from $100 to $2,000 per finished product. Product Spec's in Section two have two versions of each product. One lists a price and the other does not (in case the instructor chooses a different price or chooses not to consider price as a factor). Each product may require different raw materials (construction paper) and different construction techniques (stapling or taping instead of gluing, etc). Generally speaking, the more complex the design, the more it can be sold for, and, potentially, the more money participants can make.

If, as the customer, you want the students to try to build a certain product and they did not choose to make it, then you can raise the price you are willing to pay or simplify the design in some way. In some cases, the management team agreed to make a product only after getting cost reductions on their raw materials at Muscleman Construction. This brings up an important point; after several runs--when students become proficient--they should be allowed to negotiate price and delivery times, just as industry does it. Again, this is not a requirement; it just makes the simulation more enjoyable.

Once the management team chooses a product to make, they are "on the clock." From this point on, students in both the advanced and basic options have 30 minutes (or slightly more if you are a pushover customer as I sometimes am) to produce their products.

DESIGN TIME

In the game's most challenging version, managers choose products they want to make during the production run, then send those designs to their design engineers. These engineers then try to come up with a design that is most easily manufactured and one that makes the best use of their materials and personnel. This design time typically takes up about one-third to two-thirds of the production run time, depending on how efficient the team is.

The coordination and communication needed between design and those who must produce the product is one of the more dynamic parts of the game. Be sure to put design and manufacturing in separate sections of the room. This makes it more difficult to communicate and better simulates how it really is in industry.

If your management team designers are typical, you will find that they are usually pretty good at reducing scrap and making good use of materials, but not very good at creating designs that maximize the ability of their blue-collar production workers (e.g., require complex ability, close tolerances, etc.). Incidentally, if you doubt the ability of your students to successfully produce a product, then give them the design ahead of time and make it due the day of the production run.

An example of how to do this is seen in Figure 3. In this arrangement the students' company locates their design and manufacturing facilities on opposite sides of a normal classroom. In a tierd classroom, simply put them on opposite sides of the row.

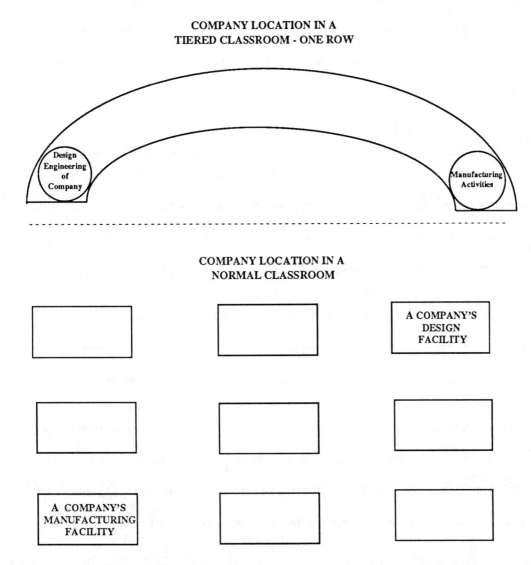

COMPANY LOCATION IN A
TIERED CLASSROOM - ONE ROW

Design
Engineering
of
Company

Manufacturing
Activities

COMPANY LOCATION IN A
NORMAL CLASSROOM

A COMPANY'S
DESIGN
FACILITY

A COMPANY'S
MANUFACTURING
FACILITY

Physically separate design and manufacturing to increase degree of communication difficulties
and realism of simulation. Primarily used when playing more advanced versions.

Figure 3

While the management's design engineers are busy designing, purchasing is responsible for procuring the necessary raw material and any new equipment needed to make a particular product. All of their materials can be purchased from Muscleman Construction, which can be run by the instructor or volunteer students. I suggest you use a student since it gives you more time to watch and analyze the production activities.

PURCHASING

In the basic option, materials are simply supplied to participants whenever they want. This is not as much of an advantage to them as it first might seem because I do not allow them to sell back any unused material. Therefore, they must count any unused material as excess inventory. Excess inventory, scrap, rework and so forth, are always measured in square inches; the less of each, the better the management.

In the advanced version, each half sheet (9" x 6") of construction paper can be purchased from the supplier, Muscleman Construction, for prices ranging from $800 to $900. Muscleman Construction can also sell thin strips of cardboard which can be used to make dies and templates for more complex products.

Purchasing must keep in mind that there is a lead time before they can receive materials. It takes approximately three minutes lead time from the moment purchasing requests supplies until they can be delivered. This helps simulate the delay that can normally be expected in the real world. As such, it encourages managers to time the flow of materials so they arrive just in time to use them.

A flow diagram of the typical transactions involved in both the basic and advanced options is seen in Figure 4. The step by step process is described in Figure 5.

MAKING THE RUN

During the actual production run, blue-collar employees (approximately five or six) are supposed to be busy cutting, gluing, taping, stenciling, drawing, measuring, inspecting, etc. If possible, it can provide an intriguing variation if participants or students from other classes are encouraged to act as employees for the management team. This gives these blue-collar employees a different perspective, since

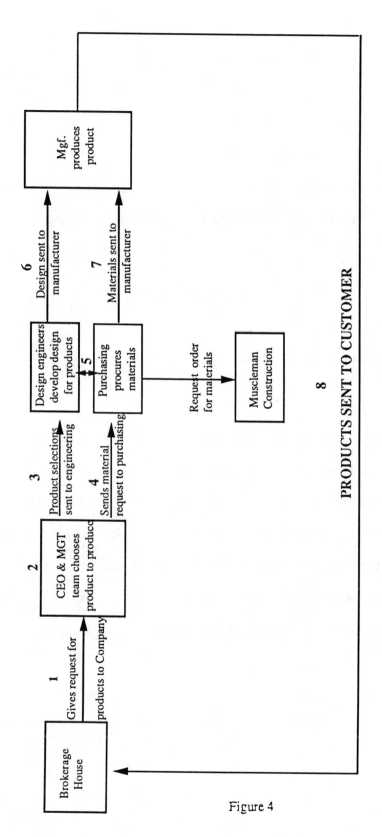

1 Gives request for products to Company

2 CEO & MGT team chooses product to produce

3 Product selections sent to engineering

4 Sends material request to purchasing

5 Design engineers develop design for products

Purchasing procures materials

6 Design sent to manufacturer

7 Materials sent to manufacturer

Mgf. produces product

Brokerage House

Request order for materials

Muscleman Construction

8 PRODUCTS SENT TO CUSTOMER

FLOW DIAGRAM OF TYPICAL TRANSACTIONS

Figure 4

STEPS IN PRODUCTION PROCESS

1. Customer, gives request for products to students company.

2. CEO and others choose products they wish to make.

3. Management sends product specifications to engineering.

4. CEO and Managers tell purchasing to procure materials from their supplier, Muscleman.

5. Purchasing procures material from supplier.

6. After engineering designs products, they are sent to manufacturing.

7. Purchasing ships materials to manufacturing.

8. Manufacturer sends finished products to customer.

All eight steps are required for advanced versions. In the basic option, the customer usually only gives the student company one product to make rather than allowing the company to choose from four or five products as in the advanced option. Since there is only one product in the basic option, there is no reason to perform step two. In the advanced option, students sell each product to their customer for different prices, so a finance manager will be needed to help decide which product is most profitable. In the basic option, price is not usually a factor. Since the focus is exclusively on production, only production, design, engineering and the CEO need to be involved in the decision.

Figure 5

they are not part of the management team. In classes, I have encouraged this by offering those students extra credit. If this is not possible, then let the production group choose its own employees and management team. Generally a group of twelve to fifteen is ideal but companies of nine can still perform well. If more than fifteen students are in the class, then divide the class into competing companies. In a large tiered classroom, make each row a company. For example, if the classroom has eight tiers, then there will be eight companies. An example of this arrangement can be see in Figure 6. An alternative way to organize companies in a school setting is by a major. Thus, there is a company of marketing, accounting, engineering, communications or other majors.

The number of workstations within a company can vary greatly. It depends on the organizational structure, type of product being produced and the ratio of direct to indirect labor. I have found that if you use a posterboard (as seen in Figure 7) to create these workstations, it not only keeps the work area cleaner, but encourages better control of materials.

PAY AND TRAINING

In the basic option, no one gets paid for his or her work. In advanced versions, employees can be paid $7.00 a minute (or any other way the management team chooses) of production time. Managers generally are paid however their CEO chooses. In some cases students have set up ESOP's, and in other cases they receive a flat salary ($300) per production period. The CEO and other managers also sometimes track how much they, and their white-collar employees, are being utilized.

Normally, the Human Resource Director, in any of the basic or advanced versions, asks employees to keep track of their "clock" or production time. He or she then collects the data, graphs and tracks the percentage of the time, and how effectively employees are being utilized. Forms and graphs for this purpose are provided in the student's instructions guide.

The advantage of tracking the percentage of time employees are being utilized is that it shows if personnel are being effectively utilized. For instance, management may discover that employees are only

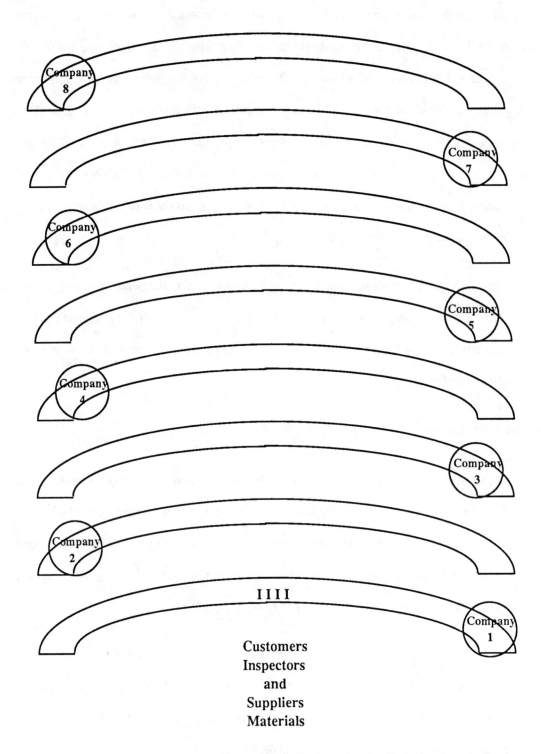

Customers
Inspectors
and
Suppliers
Materials

Diagram of where to locate companies in a large
classroom, simulating basic opiton.

Figure 6

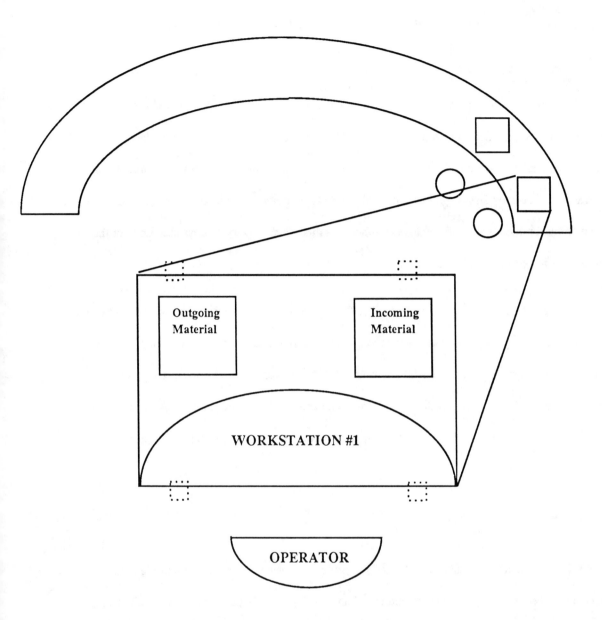

Example of a typical workstation. Take a white posterboard, cut it in four equal parts
and make each piece a workstation. Thus each posterboard can produce four
workstations. Tape workstation to desk to prevent glue or scratch marks on desk.
Outgoing and incoming material boxes also help focus students on flow of material and
possible advantages of JIT.

Figure 7

being utilized 60 percent of the time. If this is the case, they need to reorganize and improve the use of their personnel.

Hopefully, the Human Resource Director has had an orientation for employees, selected the best one for each job, and provided some training (how to cut, stencil, etc.) before beginning production. Usually student managers, at first, do not do many of these steps, like train employees, maximize employee time and so forth. As they discuss production problems that occurred, they will realize the need to better manage materials, product flow and employees' time. It is this self-discovery process that is one of the most important features of the simulation.

The student study guide has a section called "How to Win." It is based on the comments of dozens of CEO's and practicing managers, after they have watched the production runs. If these suggestions were implemented, the process would run much more smoothly. Thus, even the most novice student has some idea or objective of what to do; it's just a matter of implementation. However, for even the most seasoned practicing manager or student, execution of the plan and trying to implement a strategy will prove to be the real challenge.

EXECUTION

While the Human Resource Director is monitoring employee performance, the Production Manager should be observing what is being produced and how effectively this is occurring. Initially, Production Managers will probably get so involved in the production process that they will fail to do this. Instead, the Production Manager and the CEO will try to do it all themselves or try to explain each step as it occurs. This problem is usually resolved in the managers' meetings, after one or two production runs. The Production Manager and/or the Material Manager should be responsible for controlling material usage because excess materials, after a production run, are charged against the student's company.

In advanced versions, each company is charged $5.00 per square inch of scrap that is left at the end of a production run. The manufacturing company must also pay $10 per square inch for any raw materials, work-in-process and unsold finished goods that are left at the end of a production run. This $10 is due to holding costs that must be charged for material held from one production run to the next. (There are 54 square inches in a typical 9" x 6" half sheet of construction paper, and if students pay $800 for this sheet, then they initially pay $14.81 per square inch of new material [$800 divided by 54 = $14.81]. Charge about $5 a square inch for disposal and EPA cost for any material scrapped after each production run.

In the basic option, dollars of this overhead need not be compared (although I think it adds a bit of realism). Instead, just compare the amount of square inches of scrap, raw material, work-in-process and unsold finished goods that are left over after each production run. If you do decide to charge a holding cost for these materials, then keep it simple, say $20 of every square inch of scrap, rework, work-in-process, raw material or finished goods that remain after each production run.

The Production and Materials managers are not the only ones concerned about materials. The Quality Control Manger must also be concerned with rework and scrap, as well as drawing parts to specified dimensions since all parts must be made within one sixteenth (1/16) of an inch. If dimensions are off or other customer requirements (e.g., color, shape, construction) are not met, the lot or item is rejected. If any item in the lot is rejected, the entire shipment is returned to the manufacturer for correction or disposal. There is a mandatory three-minute delay and lead time before the lot can be resubmitted (for 100 percent inspection). If time runs out, a "nice" customer can agree to accept a shipment before it has been inspected--but if any one item in the lot fails, the whole lot is rejected and management will be charged those costs.

In advanced versions, if the company is not ready to ship at the end of the production period, a late fee is charged. If the company cannot deliver the product on time, they are assessed a late charge of 10 percent of the total selling price for the lot. If they are two minutes late, the fee is 20 percent, and three minutes cost 30 percent of the selling price. Any lot that is more than four minutes late is normally not accepted.

Of course, good as well as bad performance can be acknowledged. If the management becomes good at meeting deadlines, the instructor may choose to offer them a performance bonus of 10 percent (or any amount) of the selling price if they can deliver within 20 to 25 minutes, instead of the usual 30 minutes.

Every shipment by the manufacturing company costs them $200 (there is no cost in the basic option). As already noted, when shipments are received, they must possess either a sampling or 100 percent inspection before the manufacturer receives payment. As noted, in larger classrooms it is wise to have one volunteer from each "company" to act as incoming inspectors. Then choose a Quality Control Manager to manage the inspectors, distribute materials and keep track of incoming product. This way the instructor is free to act as an observer.

EXPECTATIONS AND GRADING

As the course continues, it is probably wise to raise customer expectations. This is one of the judgmental aspects of the game. Initially, it is a major accomplishment for most students to produce any product that meets the customer's requirements within a production cycle.

At first, it is wise to start the game off with a very simple product like a T-shaped piece, stop sign, or similar design, because it requires minimum cutting, pasting, adhering to dimensions and other managerial tasks. In the advanced version, often the second production run is where students are offered more complex, as well as simple designs to choose from.

In the basic option, the same design can be given each run because the instructor is only evaluating the students production process, not overall profitability. An alternative is to give the designs of similar difficulty, for instance, in one run an instructor might give students a yield sign (see section two) to make; the next time they might be given a stop sign or similar sign to make.

Again, judgment on the part of the instructor is required. More complex and demanding customers would be appropriate for more competent managers. Challenge, but do not break, their entrepreneurial spirit. It has been my experience that teachers tend to be a little "easy" on students at first and practitioners tend to "break" students by being too hard at first. At the end both tend to expect the same effort, completely meeting customer expectations.

In the advanced versions, grading or evaluation is based on a simple concept. If the group "meets customer requirements" they receive an A or top ranking. If they fail to meet the customer requirements, they can receive less than the A or top ranking, depending on how inefficient they were. For instance, a B or lower ranking might be given if students did not meet some of either the production or quality standards. A C or average ranking could be given if several of the requirements were not met.

As already mentioned, in basic options I focus on only one characteristic (e.g., productivity, inventory, quality, etc.) at a time because it gives me a chance to discuss those topics in detail. Examples of evaluations that have been used for both the basic and advanced version can be seen in Section four.

OVERVIEW

In its most complex or advanced version, the Production Game consists of four major parts. The first part might be called Pre-Production, and occurs in the first 10 to 20 minutes of the class. This is where the student CEO and his or her staff decide what product or products they want to produce, also where financial production and design decisions are made. Any ambiguities about the customer's design requirements, as well as negotiations about price and other requirements, occur in this period. Since in the basic option only one product is given to companies during a production run, there is only limited need for a pre-production period.

The second part of the simulation is the actual 30 minute Production Run. It starts the moment a customer's order is accepted by the management team and concludes whenever time has expired. During this time students must design the product, produce it and ship it. Inefficiencies will prolong this cycle time and cause production, quality and overhead cost problems.

The third part of this four-part process is the analysis and lasts 10 to 20 minutes depending on the length of the class. First, employees are given a chance to note what worked and did not work; then the management team gives its input. After these comments, the instructor, a guest or a "consultant" (who is usually a local plant manager or other experienced practitioner) and the classroom observers are asked to comment on what they saw. Observation sheets provided in the student's Instructions Guide and this Manual can be used to encourage participation.

In the past it has been these consultants' advice that has proved the most valuable to students. Almost every practitioner can relate the game to the real world and suggest improvements. As already noted, the game also provides guest speakers with a better medium to share their experience, since it is more informal and less intimidating than lecturing before a passive group of students.

The fourth and last part of this process is the managers' meetings. If possible, this can occur as part of the classroom activities, or it can be part of the outside classroom activities. In these meetings, students look for ways to improve their performance when another production run is made. Team members examine the numbers (e.g., labor utilization, scrap reports, quality reports, financial, etc.) to see how they did and to see how they can improve their performance numbers. Notes or videotapes of the consultant's suggestions are also discussed.

As the meeting adjourns, it might be good for the instructor to require the student CEO to summarize what changes will be made and then put that information in a report submitted to the instructor. An example of this report, called a Stockholder Report, can be seen in Section three. The report should summarize accomplishments, note changes that will be implemented before the next production run and, in the advanced versions, summarize the company's financial condition.

Instructional materials for the game include this instructor's manual as well as a students' instructions guide that describes how to play the game and, how to win and that has a section on production forms. These forms help students track production, employee utilization, quality and other measures and make it easier and more fun. Each of these forms, along with those contained in this instructor's manual, will make it easier to analyze and administer the simulation.

WHAT TO LOOK FOR

One of the real values of the game is that it reasonably mimics real-world production situations. As such, there are many real-life problems that have their parallel in the game. It is often likely that if you have become aware of or bothered about the way management is conducted in business, then you are likely to see some of the same problems arise in the game. If you have particular concerns about what it takes to be competitive in the work place today, chances are you will see these problems and solutions manifest themselves in this simulation. What many have discovered is that the simulation gives them a forum to demonstrate, explain and discuss those aspects of business, production, management and the place of the customer in organizations and the global marketplace.

The game was developed because a more dynamic way of teaching students, in a classroom setting, was needed. Productivity, quality, competition, customers, decision-making, problem-solving, risk-taking, employee involvement, participative management and communication are all dynamic concepts, but they often lose their power when presented in a lecture format. People want to do it, not just hear about it. Therefore, the simulation was created so participants could become actively involved rather than passively listening--or not listening.

In reviewing this section of the manual on what to look for, remember I am writing from a biased viewpoint. My perception of what to look for is strongly affected by my engineering, production and business background, along with a smattering of psychology. The information on these next pages is based on this background, on the insights from running it for a few years and from the insights of practicing CEO's and other managers who also had a strong production background and viewpoint.

I am sure if I had asked a person with strong communication interest or skills to observe the game, he or she would see specific problems to which most observers are blind. Just as likely, if someone watched the game who had strong beliefs in the importance of ethics, labor relations, organizational behavior or a myriad of other disciplines, I am sure that person would have new insights.

The simulation is a reasonable facsimile of reality, so you might expect to see the same problems arise in the simulation as arise in the real world. Therefore, do not just use the information on the next pages; also use your own unique insights to enlighten students. A check list of things to observe is provided at the end of this section. You might want to supplement it with ones that focus students in the direction of your interests and abilities. I also suggest that you invite outside guests to observe and comment on what they see. Choose guests who have strong viewpoints or skills in areas you wish to emphasize.

PLANNING, ORGANIZING AND STAFFING

One of the most common observations that guests have noticed when watching the game is the apparent lack of participant's application of the basic principles of management. There is often a lack of good planning and organization in both initially organizing and running the companies. Often the participants' first impulse is to "hit the ground running" rather than to spend the necessary preliminary time planning and organizing how the company will be organized and run. Obviously, this should occur before, not after, work has started.

Although participants have their Instruction and Study Guide that emphasizes the need for better organization (see the How to Win section of their booklet), they tend to overlook even the most basic organizational considerations. In my classes, I always give participants a class period in which to organize their company, but it will take more than 40 or 50 minutes to come up with an effective organization.

If possible they should be encouraged to have a meeting outside class and before the first production run. Despite this encouragement, I have never run the simulation when participants did not make significant changes in their organizational structure after their first production run. This is good and it gives them a chance to create an organization that is effective and not one that they think the teacher wants them to create. The instructor should encourage this frequent reassessment; otherwise students may never develop an effective organization and may just get by--not unlike many counterparts in real life companies.

ORGANIZING A COMPANY

Organizational behavior types would have a field day watching most participants trying to organize how to best do the job at hand. Obviously, designing an organization that is best suited to producing their products is of critical importance. During this process students should be analyzing the product they plan to make and deciding how to do it. This process helps them focus the organization on achieving those objectives. At the very least, they should try to specifically identify responsibilities and specific accountabilities of each team member.

Time spent initially organizing a company will greatly enhance students' ability to do their job, but instructors should not force them to do anything, including initial organizing. The real power of the game is having students make mistakes, pull themselves up by their bootstraps and go back at it again. Remember, they are not simply left to sink or swim. Their Study Guide gives them plenty of hints about both organizing and running a company. They probably heard many of the concepts before this class exercise.

Despite all of this "input," students will usually not organize at all (e.g., Who does what? Who reports to whom?), or they use a generic organizational structure rather than one uniquely suited to their particular situation. However, in this case they will learn and they will reorganize. Here, as in business, it is not memorization that matters--it's performance. If they do not organize so that they can perform, they will lose their customer and lose to their competition.

VOLUME VS. LAYOUT

Instructors will want to notice, beyond simple organizational considerations, whether the participants' organizations are designed to do the right job. Often students set up organizations and create a production layout for a repetitive or assembly line organization when they are actually producing a job shop product. Of course, the reverse is also true; they could set up a job shop when they are actually operating in a repetitive environment.

Generally speaking, if the management team is only making one product, with long production runs, they should organize an assembly line company. If they are making two or more products with small lot sizes, say between 5 and 25, then they should organize a job shop company. In situations where the team is supposed to be making a small run of a product, they might want to consider just training one person to do the entire assembly job rather than setting up an entire plant to handle one item with a short production run.

The students' Study Guide stresses the need to balance work and flow of products. Instructors will want to watch the number of workstations being set up and compare them to the number of products the students are supposed to produce. For instance, if the company only needs to make ten products but the management team has set up six workstations, then the company cannot effectively produce the product. There simply is not enough work to keep all the stations busy. Management should either reduce the number of workstations or increase the volume of work.

So far the discussion has only been about low volume problems. Problems can also arise when there is too great a volume, or too great a variation in volume for the way the company is organized. If the company has set up six workstations to perform six production steps that are necessary to produce a product, things should be OK as long as the volume does not vary greatly from one work center to the next.

If workstations one, two and three each take 45 seconds to perform their task, then work should flow smoothly (assuming no breakdowns). However, if one of the three steps takes two minutes instead of forty-five seconds, then there will be a bottleneck at that work station. One solution would be to subdivide the work so time is again equally spaced. Management could also add more workstations or more people. There is no rule that says they must have one job step for one person. Two, three or more people can work at a single workstation.

CHOOSING THE RIGHT PERSON

One organizational aspect that is often overlooked is selecting personnel. Instructors should note if the company has the right employees, as well as managers assigned to the right jobs. Some people tend to get so nervous or tense that they fail to do a job. If the job is critical then the company is in trouble.

Some employees just do not have the training or, sometimes, the capacity to do certain jobs. Believe it or not, some people cannot even cut a straight line, or print neatly. If this is the case they should not be in key positions. Just because someone wants to do a particular job does not mean she or he will be good at it. Instructors should encourage students to develop skills tests, like the example in their booklet, before choosing people to perform certain jobs. Skills tests should also be developed for some management personnel.

A good engineering designer is critical to reducing scrap and rework because he or she must figure out the best way to place an item on a 6" by 9" sheet of construction paper so little excess scrap remains. Likewise, if design comes up with a poor design, they are building in the risk of greater rework and scrap because employees simply cannot do what design wants them to do. Designers also must be able to set up the production process so the company can make the best use of their employees' skills and time. (Some designs require excessive measuring, close tolerance and high skill from employees.)

The designer job is a popular choice among students. It is fun and has plenty of status. However, it is a job that requires specialized abilities. To be a good designer, one must be able to think or visualize an item in three dimensions. All good designers can visually see an object, turn it around in their head, and come up with an acceptable design.

Good designers must also be very creative. They need to think divergently. They need to be good problem solvers. Sometimes they may even need to draw well. Students should be careful who they place in this, and other key positions.

OPTIONS

Instructors can decide to give students several designs to choose from rather than giving them only one. When this occurs, additional factors can be considered. Personally, I think the initial design selection process is one of the more exciting parts of the game. With more than one design to choose from, management has to decide which one is more producible and/or profitable.

To choose the best design, management usually assembles a team (if they are smart) consisting of the CEO, designers and production managers. Finance managers are also part of the team if profits are a factor in choosing the best design.

Instructors should allow about ten to fifteen minutes for this product selection process. The process of choosing a product is a delicate balance. There is a need for some input from key managers, but it is possible to go overboard with this and suffer from "paralysis through analysis." If an effective decision cannot be made, reassess and reorganize.

CONTROLLING, DIRECTING AND LABOR RELATIONS

Management in the game and in real life needs a certain amount of detachment. The students' Study Guide emphasizes that the most common mistake made by management, especially the CEO, is to end up doing the employee's job. Managers cannot manage if they are doing blue-collar work. The management team should be checking to see how things are going and correcting problems as they arise. Practitioners observing the game always seem to note that this correcting of problems as they occur, is how the Japanese were able to out produce America.

Certainly managers of companies in the simulation should be checking to see how things are going because they must be able to halt and correct problems as they arise. Often, however, managers in the game and in business are so busy "fighting fires" that they never get ahead of the problem. If managers have to do the employees' job, then employees were not trained well enough. Better training will eliminate many of the fires that these managers feel compelled to "manage."

Instead of just managing to get by, managers should show signs of good planning. One example of this is a good preventative maintenance program. If, during the production process, managers discover broken parts, glue sticks that are dried out, pencils or other equipment that is worn out, dull or not ready for production, then a preventative maintenance program is desperately needed. Most "fires" are caused, and preventative maintenance is often the cure. Other cures include a good orientation program for employees and good training and motivational programs.

COMMUNICATION

A great number of problems within the production system of companies occur because of poor communication between managers and their employees. It is essential for the company CEO and other managers to give good reasons why decisions were made. If the CEO chooses a particular product to make over other possibilities, then he or she should explain why the decision was made. Others do not have to agree, but at least they should be informed. People want to know why they are doing the things they are doing. It sounds simple, but if it is common sense, then why is it not common practice?

In the game and in business when you have a design department that receives product requests, designs them and then gives them to production so they can be produced, there is always the risk of poor communication. Because it is so easy to have these communication breakdowns, it is often wise to have a liaison between production and design.

If communication is good between production and design, then nothing needs correcting. However, if it can be improved, then a process planner might be used. This liaison talks to both production and design about what products and tools are needed to do the job. Sometimes this person develops a flow chart that shows the proposed layout (e.g., product goes from drawing, to cutting and so forth) and estimates the time it takes to do the job.

One sign of good communication, other than a smoothly running organization, is the effective use of the product specifications to assess a proposed product's impact on each person's job. Manufacturing and quality control obviously will want access to the spec sheets. Manufacturing will need to determine how to produce the product and who is to do what so it best meets the customers' requirements. Quality control could use the product specification sheets to identify their quality inspection check points. Human resources might also want to use the prints for training and skills assessment (e.g., Is neat printing involved? etc.).

Another means of improving communication is to improve prototypes. If a product is difficult to make, it is sometimes wise for design engineers to make a prototype of the product. Design engineering then sits down with production personnel and shows them what to do in order to meet customer expectations.

IMPROVING LABOR PERFORMANCE

Controlling direct and indirect labor costs and making the best possible use of the employee's time is important because it is a major overhead cost in any business. Management does not want to have 100 percent direct labor utilization because it does not leave time for indirect activities like training, scheduling, maintenance and so on. Nevertheless, it is important to have most of your employees directly involved in producing products (or services) rather than being sidetracked with excessive indirect activities. Obviously, it is worse still to have significant idle time among the workforce.

While in industry many companies try for direct labor utilization of 80 to 85 percent, it is wise to expect labor utilization percentages in the game in the range of around 92 to 95 percent. This higher percentage is reasonable since the simulation simplifies employee activities needed to do work. In the game, if employees are not working on the line producing a product, then they are probably idle and that is worse that having them distracted in indirect labor activities.

To reach the mid-nineties in terms of labor utilization, managers will have to keep most of their blue-collar employees busy most of the time during an actual production run. Do not count pre-production activities like training time against direct labor utilization figures. It will be enough of a challenge for most managers just to keep them productive during a production run. You will probably find that their labor utilization figures at first will be in the mid-fifties or lower, not mid-nineties.

For these managers to have any hope of managing their employees' time and focusing in on corrective measures, they must be able to measure both the amount and time spent working. Without a means of measuring employee performance they will not even be aware of a problem, much less know how to solve it. Once they realize there is a problem with employee time and productivity at various workstations, they can correct the problem by decentralizing, reorganizing, changing accountabilities and responsibilities or a wide range of other managerial options. Recognition of the problem is the key step.

For this reason, it is critical to the functioning of the game that participants be encouraged to use the performance measurement forms in their guidebook. Clock in/out data and other labor utilization forms give students tools to identify problems. As the old adage goes, "If you can't measure it, you can't manage it." Although I do not believe it is wise for any instructor to coerce students into using any of the material, instructors should strongly encourage use of these forms. It gives both you and your students something to discuss and provides a forum for showing them ways to make better use of their personnel.

MANAGERIAL AND LABOR UTILIZATION

It is also wise to encourage the organization to closely monitor their managers', as well as employees', time that is spent working and not working. The labor utilization reports and forms can be used for managers as well as for employees. Whether informally or formally, encourage student managers to keep good records of the time each person is working; then summarize those findings and compare them to previous runs and to the competition's utilization. They may find surprises. As their guidebook notes, one company did this analysis and found that their CEO worked 45 minutes, quality control 30 minutes, and material management and all other managers and employees were only working 15 minutes. This company obviously needed to, and did, reorganize.

The need for using labor (and managerial) utilization forms has already been noted. Flow charts are another way of improving labor utilization as well as improving inventory control. Flow charts can help because they identify the steps involved in producing a product and then estimate how long each step should take before production actually begins. Tracking a job's beginning, ending and key steps in between also improves efficiency because you are able to more quickly stop bottlenecks that might occur. Since flow charts show the number of workstations needed and how long each should and does take, they provide problem identification as well as a problem-solving tool.

Other means of improving labor utilization and other resources include the possibility of measuring the percentage of time equipment is being utilized. If certain equipment is being under- or over-utilized, it can often be the source of labor utilization problems. Instituting flextime (stagger time employees work), teaching employees multi-skills and better scheduling also improves labor management.

LABOR RELATIONS

The real measure of management's ability to communicate and manage is its relationship with the employees. Students and practicing managers have been told, probably since the first management course, about the need to effectively utilize their most potent resource--their people. Despite these urgings, employees remain an under-utilized resource in most organizations. In spite of similar urgings in the students' Study Guide, often instructors will find that most participants in the game will still fail to make good use of their employees' time, hearts and minds.

Labor utilization reports and forms, in the students' Study Guide, only help measure and manage one of these three--time. Those reports measure the percentage of employees' time that is being utilized, not the percentage of their minds and hearts that is being utilized. This provides fertile ground for discussion and analysis.

Employee involvement is of increasing importance in a competitive marketplace. Instructors should check to see if the management team is getting sincere input from their employees. A simple employee attitude survey is provided in the Study Guide. As the students' guide shows, many significant improvements in the operation of the company and in producing products came about because of employee insights and suggestions.

One example in the student's guidebook notes how an employee improved both quality and productivity by making a layout change that only an employee would be aware of. Such insights are not surprising; after all, employees even in this simulation, are the ones who best know what their tools and equipment are and are not capable of doing. One of the values of the game is that students cannot just read about employee involvement and forget it. To be effective against their competition, they will have to react, and get everyone solving problems, not just the CEO.

QUALITY CONTROL AND MANAGEMENT

Employee involvement is one of the keys to producing higher quality products. Often what students fail to realize is that quality cannot be inspected in; it has to be built in from the start. Frequent inspections simply help catch mistakes early, not prevent them. Notwithstanding, this inspection is still an important part of controlling the quality of products.

Students usually have end-of-the line inspectors, but sometimes fail to have in-process inspections. Of course the ideal approach would be for management to train employees so the employees are their own inspectors. Doing away with managerial inspection and relying on employee inspection requires a great deal of trust, not to mention training. In many businesses this managerial trust is rare. It will be interesting to see if your students have this trust and insight.

Related to the need for inspection is something often called a first-piece check. Every good production process does a first-piece check. It was the most common suggestion made by practitioners who watched production runs. A first-piece check involves inspecting the first piece, first part, first sub-assembly, or first assembly of a product to make sure it is being built successfully.

More than once a company has made the mistake of initially marking or laying out a product wrong, but not finding out until several products, sometimes not even before a entire lot, is rejected. It would be unwise to check every item in such detail, because companies would spend more time inspecting than producing, but an initial first-piece check is always a good idea.

When inspecting products, students often take the narrow view. They only check to make sure that the 1/16 inch or smaller tolerance on all pieces is not being violated. They frequently overlook the fact that the customer wants the product to be well constructed so it will not fall apart. Customers also want it to look attractive--no smudges or marks, and they want it neatly lettered. Quality is all these, and whatever else, the customer considers important.

One of the best preventative measures concerning quality, inventory or any other manageable area is for students to question the process. Stop immediately when they discover a problem and fix it on the spot. The sooner the process occurs, the better the organization.

QUALITY IS MORE THAN INSPECTION

As already noted here and in the student's guidebook, you cannot simply inspect quality into products--it has to be build in. Chance variations will occur in any process. The trick is to reduce them to a minimum and control all assignable or non-chance variations. It is possible for each piece of a product to be in control and for the entire product to be out of control. That is because there are normal variations when anything is made. If these normal variations all accumulate in one direction, then it could make the entire product fall outside product speculations.

These chance variations are not as much of a quality problem as assignable causes of variation. Assignable causes of variation in product quality can be due to using the wrong method or materials, poor training, faulty equipment, or a dozen other reasons.

Inspectors should emphasize that good design is the key to good production. It can help control both assignable and chance causes of variation. Too tight a tolerance on parts and creating parts or pieces that are too difficult to make, are mistakes that are designed in at the beginning. Designers can create

almost any design, but if the equipment and talents are not available to do the job, the design is a poor one.

Sometimes designers assume they can get a "factory edge" (squared, smooth edge), but that may not be

possible and the production process will create more scrap than the designers thought.

Good design is not the only way to insure quality. Templates and dies also reduce inspection and

help design in quality because they reduce the skills needed to do inspection work. Dies or templates also

improve the speed, as well as quality, of a production process. Rather than each inspector tediously

checking the measurements of sides, lengths, and other characteristics of a product, like stop signs, it would

be easier to just draw out the shape on a scrap of paper and lay a finished product down on top of the

diagram or template to see if it passes or not. If it fits, they have made a good product. If it is longer,

shorter or whatever, then they have a quality problem.

Today, customers are more demanding. They want to get away from having to inspect the quality

of products being shipped from their suppliers. They just want to pick the product up and use it, without

incoming inspection. They want to know that the products they get from their suppliers are right and that

if those items are not, then the supplier is liable for damages. As the instructor, and the students' customer,

you may want to institute these stronger perspectives after they have become reasonably proficient at

producing a good product. A later section discusses this customer perspective in greater detail.

INVENTORY CONTROL

"How much?" and "When?" are the two major inventory questions. How much inventory is

needed to just insure that the product is produced, and when this inventory is needed are two questions

students must answer. Increasingly, industry has been lowering both of these numbers. Often inventory

items have gone from economic order quantities to a just-in-time (JIT) philosophy. Management has been

moving from producing large lots, with ample safety stock, toward attempting to produce lots that approach

a lot size of one.

JIT, or a pull system of inventory, is a powerful way to reduce inventory as well as increase the speed of the production process. Most students will use the traditional push rather than this pull system. As such, they keep trying to shove materials from one work station to the next. This tends to cause bottlenecks and increase the amount of work-in-process inventory, as well as increase the amount of rework. When they use the pull system, a workstation only gives the next work area what they request, not what the workstation produces-as in the push system.

In the production game, as in industry, the objective is to reduce inventory overhead costs. These costs can account for 70 to 80 percent of a typical manufacturer's overhead. Reducing this overhead greatly enhances competitiveness. It also improves the flow of goods.

The smaller the lot size, the smoother the flow of materials and products. If a product is moving from one workstation to the next and the lot size is ten, then ten items must be completed at each workstation before the lot can be moved to the next workstation.

The ideal way to manage inventory is to produce in lots of one--thereby reducing waiting time, in-process inventory and excess materials. For instance, if you have five workstations and lots of ten, then your maximum items in the production system is fifty (5 x 10 = 50). On the other hand, if you again had five workstations but this time had lots of one, then the maximum in the system would be five (5 x 1 = 5). Obviously, this is a simplified explanation, but it does make the point that reductions in inventory throughout the system saves materials, time and labor.

Obviously, I am a proponent of JIT, but I do not believe in coercion of students. If they do not want to implement JIT, they should not be forced to do so. Instead, I have found if you emphasize the benefits of JIT and make it easy for them to visualize the process, they are more likely to implement it! One way of doing this is to set up work stations that accentuate the concept of inventory. To do this, I develop a cardboard workstation similar to that seen earlier in Figure 7.

The workstation has a place for incoming and outgoing material. Students are encouraged to put appropriate materials in these boxes. The workstation's semi-circle is where the actual work is performed.

From a practical standpoint, the cardboard workstation also helps keep a neater desk and prevents glue and cut marks getting on the desk. A regular piece of cardboard will make four work centers.

While emphasizing the benefits of JIT and the use of the cardboard workstations will help students control inventory, it is not the complete answer. Control of inventory requires more than producing in small lots. Managers must constantly be checking up and down the line to see how many components and finished products are being produced. Monitoring work flow, along with monitoring the queue time at the customer's incoming inspection and keeping track of the time remaining is extremely important. Everything else is planning. This is execution of the plan. It is both the plan and execution of the plan that reduces work-in-process and inventory levels and increases quality and productivity.

CUSTOMER ATTENTION

One of the truly realistic aspects of the simulation is how the customer takes center stage in the production process. Customers may not always be right, but they are right unless there is clear proof that they are wrong; the burden of proof rests with management. As has become painfully clear, many U.S. companies have lost market share because they failed to keep close contact with their customers. Successful companies in the future will focus on total customer satisfaction.

Students, like many managers, often do not appreciate the center place that customers maintain in the typical successful company. Many mistakes in the game are made because management did not thoroughly question their customer. Management should never assume they understand their customers. They must constantly question and keep close contact with them; otherwise they cannot give them what they want.

In business, it is not uncommon for management to not meet the customer's requirements because what the customer wanted was not on the specification sheet. The same is true of the game. Most students will question those things on the product specification sheet that they do not understand, but unfortunately, that is where they stop. Even finding out what the customer does not want is not enough.

If students question and discover that their customer does not want a product made a certain way, they have only halfway done their job. They still do not know what their customer does want. Finding out what the customer does not want and what he or she does want are two entirely different things. In the students' Study Guide, this exact situation was mentioned. In this case the customer wanted some lettering on a sign using cut out or stenciled black letters. The student managers asked if they could use pencil instead of stencil letters and the customer said "No." The managers dropped the issue and did not pursue the investigation (they also produced a poor product). They should have asked the customer if there were any other lettering possibilities. If they had, they would have discovered that the dark black color was what the customer was really interested in, and not the stencil. The customer would have readily agreed to printing in a black felt-tip pen (its letters are darker than pencil); in fact, he would have supplied the equipment if the students had only inquired.

ALWAYS MAINTAINING CLOSE CONTACT

The management team must always maintain close contact <u>during</u> the production run as well as <u>before</u> production begins. They need to contact their customer before the production begins so they can clear up any misunderstanding. The management team should tell their customer who they are (designers, other managers of a company), and find out if their customer likes the work they have done in the past. In these meetings they should try to discover both their customer's perception as well as expectation of the quality of their products and service. The idea is to beat the competition by being better informed.

It is also wise during the actual production run for management to sometimes visit their customer rather than watching every detail of the production run. The objective is to again find out if their customer is satisfied with the products they have been receiving. Remember, for a time customers may accept products, but not really be satisfied with them.

CRISIS MANAGEMENT

When problems with delayed schedules do occur, the company CEO should let their customer know what is happening. In most cases, customers are fairly understanding when they know what is going on. Of course, if the company keeps telling the customer they are going to deliver and then do not, their customer will lose faith in that company.

This brings up an important point. When the instructor (or customer) has several companies making products and then gives a time at the end of the production run for students to turn in their work, some may still be waiting in line (behind other companies) at an inspection station when time runs out. One way to handle this situation is to agree to accept the lot, but let them know that if the customer finds one defective product in the lot, the entire lot will be rejected and it will be counted as scrap.

Negotiation is part of any real supplier-customer relationship. As the customer, you can decide how much negotiation will be possible in your exercise. Students should never assume that no negotiation is possible, unless you tell them so. Some instructors will let students ship in partial lots; others will not. Sometimes customers offer a performance bonus if the products are delivered early to them. Sometimes customers or instructors do not offer a performance bonus. Sometimes prices or delivery times of raw materials and/or finished goods are a negotiable subject, and at other times they are not. Managers, good managers at least, will find out what the limits are--they will think creatively.

CHECK LIST

The following two check lists summarize some of the key considerations to note when assessing student performance. They are not complete lists and should be supplemented with those concerns of each individual instructor. The check lists can be given to students or to outside guests, or they can be strictly used by the instructor. The first check list or the second can be used in part or broken down so that only one subject area is analyzed each time a production run is made.

The first check list is organized into the following categories: Planning and Organizing, Staffing, Controlling and Directing Labor Relations, Quality Control, Inventory, and Customer. It has been used when instructors were analyzing productivity, production, inventory, quality and other cost considerations. This check list has been specifically used in production and operations management courses and industrial technology and engineering courses.

The second check list is organized into the following categories: Planning, Operational Level Planning, Organizing, Control and Cost Consciousness. This check list has been used in supervisory and management courses. As already noted, each instructor should also supplement these check lists with concepts he or she is also trying to emphasize.

PLANNING AND ORGANIZING

Planning	Does it appear that management decided what type of layout and product they would make before they organized their company?	YES/NO
Planning	Are there indications of poor planning or poor preventive maintenance (e.g., dried out glue stick, broken pencils, lost materials, staplers not working)?	YES/NO
Planning	Did management draw a flow chart or use some other method to show how and where their product begins, ends and its key steps?	YES/NO
Planning/ Organization	If students are given a choice in selecting a design, are both design engineers and production and other relevant managers involved in selecting the product?	YES/NO
Planning/ Organization	Did their production system have too few or too many workstations?	YES/NO
Organization	Do key managers use the product specification sheet to help better manage their job?	YES/NO
Organization	Was the company organized in a job shop format when they should have organized in a repetitive operation (or vice versa)?	YES/NO
Organization	Does it appear that management knows who is accountable to whom?	YES/NO
Organization	Did the management team suffer from "paralysis through analysis?"	YES/NO

STAFFING

Staffing	Did management assign specific duties to specific personnel?	YES/NO
Planning/ Staffing	Do Human Resources or other managers discuss where they are going to get the personnel and what skills and training are needed to produce the product?	YES/NO
Staffing	Are the right people, with the necessary skills assigned to the jobs that best suit them (pay attention to managerial jobs (CEO, designers, etc.) as well as employees?	YES/NO
Staffing (Orientation)	Do employees practice their job before work starts?	YES/NO
Staffing (Orientation)	Was there an orientation process for new employees?	YES/NO
Staffing (Training)	Is there evidence of good training (employees know their job and have the necessary skills to do the job)?	YES/NO

CONTROLLING & DIRECTING

Control	Is management measuring their performance; do they need more measures (the more measurement, the better so they can evaluate their performance)?	YES/NO
Directing	Does the CEO or other manager explain why they made a decision, or do they simply expect their order to be followed?	YES/NO
Directing	Are production plans clearly communicated to employees (may need written specification for products)?	YES/NO
Directing	Are the CEO and other managers observing instead of doing the work of employees?	YES/NO
Directing	Are managers correcting problems as they occur or are they ignoring them?	YES/NO
Directing (Worker)	Does management involve employees in solving problems before production begins?	YES/NO
Directing (Worker)	Does management involve employees in problem solving during production?	YES/NO
Directing (Worker)	Does the Human Resource or other managers ask employees what type of equipment they need to do the job?	YES/NO
Directing (Comm.)	Were there personality clashes or conflicts?	YES/NO
Directing (Comm.)	Was there good communication between design and manufacturing?	YES/NO

LABOR RELATIONS

Planning	Did managers do a good job scheduling work?	YES/NO
Controlling	Does management monitor how well employees are working during a production run?	YES/NO
Controlling	Is management measuring their employee performance?	YES/NO
Controlling	Does management keep good records of work and non-work time?	YES/NO
Directing	Is management effectively utilizing employees? (What percentage of the time is each employee working during a production run?)	YES/NO
Directory	Is management itself being properly utilized? (What percentage of time is each manager working during a production run?)	YES/NO
Directing	Does the company use flextime?	YES/NO
Directing	Do they have multi-skilled employees?	YES/NO
Directing	Does management train well enough that employees are able to do their job?	YES/NO

QUALITY CONTROL

Planning	Are there indications that management tried to design in quality rather than simply inspect it in?	YES/NO
Controlling	Does management have in-process inspectors as well as end-of-the-line inspectors?	YES/NO
Controlling	Do employees check their own work?	YES/NO
Controlling	Do employees check their work at the end of each assembly point?	YES/NO
Controlling	Did management do a first-piece check (checked first piece, first assembly, etc.)?	YES/NO
Controlling	Are they inspecting other characteristics other than just meeting the 1/16" requirement (e.g., appearance, etc.)?	YES/NO
Controlling	Does management use a die or template to draw the shape of the product they are making (makes it easier to inspect)?	YES/NO
Controlling	Does management stop immediately when they have a quality control problem and fix it on the spot?	YES/NO
Controlling	Do you feel the company's customer needs inspectors (because the company produces poor quality) to check the quality of incoming products?	YES/NO

INVENTORY

Planning	What effect did the lot size have on production?	YES/NO
Planning	Was the lot size fairly small?	YES/NO
Planning/ Organizing	If appropriate, did management implement JIT or use another way to reduce inventory, work-in-process, etc.?	YES/NO
Planning/ Organizing Directing	Did management have enough inventory to do the job? Why?	YES/NO
Control	Was management monitoring down the line to see how many components, parts and products they had to ship at the end of the production run?	YES/NO

CUSTOMER

Directing	Does management maintain close contact with their customer?	YES/NO
Directing	Does management question the customer on anything they are unclear about (e.g., product specification)?	YES/NO
Directing	Does management do a good job of finding alternative methods of producing a product?	YES/NO
Directing	Does management contact customers before a production run with any questions they have?	YES/NO
Directing	Does management contact their customer during a production run with any questions they have?	YES/NO
Directing	Does management compare customer perceptions to customer expectations about their products?	YES/NO
Directing	If problems occur does management contact the customer?	YES/NO
Directing	Does management try to negotiate price, delivery, etc.?	

PLANNING CONSIDERATIONS

1.   Did it look like the company had clearly defined what it was trying to do?
      -Would measurable objectives have helped?

2.   Did they need any policies that would have helped run the organization?
      *Policies make it easier to delegate. Was there ample delegation?

3.   Do they need to develop any procedures that improve performance (usually specifics about how work is done)?
      *Procedure for how work is to be done.
      *Who is to do what job, and skills needed for job.
      *Scheduling of work flow.

4.   Do they need to develop a standardized method of work (cut on line)?
      -Ask problem solving approach.
      -Look for high labor cost, high scrap, waste.

5.   Are there any rules which should be instituted that would improve performance?

OPERATIONAL LEVEL PLANNING CONSIDERATIONS

1.   Is equipment doing its job? What equipment would do job better?

2.   Have they found the best method of doing work?
     -Use flow chart.
     -Effective work methods.

3.   Did they make the best use of space?

4.   Did they make effective use of materials and supplies (or was there a lot of scrap and rework)?

5.   Did they (managers) manage their own time effectively?

ORGANIZING CONSIDERATIONS

1.   Was there a clear unity of command while the company operated?
     -Did everyone know their job duties and responsibilities?

2.   Was there effective use and development of people (supervision of people was effective)?
     -Span of control.
     -Performance standards.
     -Were the right people assigned to the right job (design, front line employees)?

3.   Did line and staff work well together? Did each know their authority and responsibility?

4.   Was there effective delegation of authority?
     -Granting authority, assigning responsibilities, required accountability.

5.   Why didn't they delegate more responsibility (inspection)?
     -Afraid of employee mistakes.
     -Do not want to give up power.
     -Unsure.
     -Immature employees.

6.   Did managers choose effective understudies (employees)?
     -Did they develop them?
     -Do they reward them (incentive)?

CONTROL CONSIDERATIONS

1.   Did they set up any preliminary controls?
        -Preventive maintenance.
        -Disciplinary rules.

2.   Were there any in-process controls?
        -Check on progress midway through.
        -Were they measuring quality/quantity?

3.   Was there any evidence of effective setting of standards?
        -Physical.
        -Monetary.
        -Time.

4.   Were there any points that needed more control?
        -Scrap.
        -Rework.
        -Absenteeism.

5.   Did management have any effective use of performance standards?
        -Were they good standards?

6.   Was there indication that management was checking their performance against work standards by:
        -personal observation,
        -reports (% of scrap, etc.),
        - spot checks.

7.   Was any corrective action necessary when standards of performance were not being met?

COST CONSCIOUSNESS

1.   Did managers overmanage or practice management-by-exception?

2.   Did managers appear cost conscious?

3.   Did employees appear cost conscious?

4.   Did management enlist the help and cooperation of employees in trying to control expenses?

5.   Did management set objectives and define specific results they expected?

SECTION II

PRODUCT SPECIFICATION SHEETS

This section of the manual contains the Engineering and Production Specifications sheets that are used in running both the advanced and basic options of the simulation. In essence, these diagrams are simple blueprints of the products requested by the students' customer. The instructor, acting as this customer, assigns or lets students choose which product or products they wish to produce.

Notice that there are two versions of each of these product designs. The first design simply describes the product. The second one, of the same design, also describes the product and identifies a suggested price that the customer agrees to pay for the product. If you are concerned about emphasizing profitability as well as productivity (as in advanced versions), then the second one, that identifies price, is the one to use. Several blank product specification sheets are also provided in case the instructor wishes to create his/her own designs.

Each of these sheets has a box in the lower right-hand corner. It lists the name of the customer, the Brokerage House, the name of the item to be produced, the amount needed, its due date (in minutes) and any special notes about the product. The amount needed, due date and any special notes, can be used to change the way products are produced.

As can be seen, the instructor has three decisions to make. These decisions include how many of each product will be needed, the lot size that will be shipped to the customer, and when you, the customer, will need them. In the advanced versions, instructors will also need to decide how much they are willing to pay for them.

AMOUNT NEEDED

The amount of products needed during a production run is the first question each instructor must answer. It is easiest, during a production run, for students to produce as much as they can within the 30 minute production run. This is often the way I do it during a production run, when I am using the basic option in a large classroom.

The alternative to this situation is to request only a small lot size, say between 5 to 20 of each item. This format is especially appropriate when: trying to simulate a job shop (that produces a variety of products), working with a small class, dealing with students who have good management skills, or when using the advanced version where profits per run are being considered.

LOT SIZE

The lot size is the amount that student companies can ship at any one time. Again, the easiest is to ship in any amount. However, this detracts from the realism of the game. Real customers would not want

to be receiving various size shipments from their supplier at any time of day. Management of the manufacturing firm also could not afford to ship in extremely small amounts, with partial truckloads or with excessive variations in shipping time; therefore, instructors need to establish realistic lot sizes.

If you are unsure about the students' ability to successfully produce products, then set the lot sizes in single digits. For instance, the triangle product shown on one of the specification sheets might be shipped in lots between five to nine. The instructor's volunteer students, who act as incoming quality inspectors, would check each shipment of five or six, or whatever amount comes in, to make sure it meets the customer's requirements. Incidentally you should have about one inspector for every company. For instance, if four companies are competing for incoming products to the customer.

If you are using the basic option with everyone or every team making the same product and competing with each other, then ask that all shipments be a specific lot size. It makes the game easier to administer. You might also consider setting the lot size small, say five, when everyone is first learning the game, then later increasing the lot sizes for products when they gain more ability and experience.

In job shop settings or the advanced versions, always have fairly small lot sizes (5 to 25) since it requires better planning skills. Usually, the more complex the product, the smaller the lot size, since it is more difficult to produce the more complex designs.

Listed in Figure 8 are some of the product amounts needed, their lot size, and any time restrictions (when needed) that might apply. These amounts should not be considered recommendations. They are simply amounts I requested of my students in a job shop situation, where they had some experience and where they were making at least two products during a production run. Their objective was to maximize profits as well as productivity.

Usually the triangle, hour glass shape or other simple (no assembly) item is used for making practice runs. The I-brace, T-shape, stop, yield and warning signs have been used in both the basic and advanced versions, as well as job shop and repetitive operations. In the basic option, repetitive arrangements simply have the students produce as many of one of those products as they can within a 30 minute period. I had students ship all lots in batches of five. This repetitive arrangement greatly improves their speed and ability to deliver products. So make sure there are enough inspectors to check incoming shipments. When the instructor allows students to design how the product will best fit on their one-half sheet of construction paper outside of class, and focus exclusively on producing as many good products as they can within the 30 minute production period, then their speed greatly improves. (Usually in-class design time, during a production run, will take 10 to 20 minutes of the 30 minute production period.) It is easy to see how the number of products they can produce would increase.

FOR YOUR CONSIDERATION

Most of the product specification sheets are self explanatory, but some deserve special mention. For instance, the special note about the T-shaped piece states that it should be built in "two different colors." When students read this, they may <u>assume</u> the horizontal part of the piece is supposed to be red (or

JOB SHOP LOTS & AMOUNTS

PRODUCT	AMOUNT (shipped to customer)	LOT SIZE (in minutes)	TIME
Triangle	10	10	20 (Rush)
Hour Glass	8	8	30
I-Brace	25	12 (min. lot size)	30
T-Shape	20	20	30
Paper Chain	36	36	30
Rectangle Flags	15	15	30
Walk/Don't Walk	30	30	30
Problem Solving	10	10	30
Stop Signs	10	10	20 (Rush)
Yield Signs	20	20	30
Warning Signs	10	10	30
Road Signs	10	10	30
Road Barrier	8	(any amount)	30
Bridge Barrier	12	12	30
Three-way Sign	15	3 (min. lot size)	25 (Rush)
"Noble" Gate	10	10	30
Basketball Goal (without net-- was subcontracted out)	30	8	30
Barrel (students developed & deter- mined how many they could produce	15	15	30

Figure 8

some other color) and that the vertical piece should be blue or vice versa. If they do not ask their customer which pieces are red and which are blue, they are making a mistake. Management should never assume; they should find out by questioning their customer. Assuming, rather than finding out the customer's requirements, is one of the most common mistakes made in the early production runs.

With the paper chain or other items, it is possible to use different construction methods other than gluing. They might be riveted (stapled), taped, or clipped together. The point is, as the simulation continues, keep challenging them with new twists.

One of the most difficult production jobs for student employees to do in the game is to write or print neatly. Whenever there is lettering involved in producing a product, as it is with most signs like stop and yield signs, there is always the risk of production problems. The need to letter neatly, defined as "legal lettering" on some of the products, has and will cause many to have a meltdown.

As the instructor, you have several choices. First, you can just let it happen. Students should have realized that when dealing with complicated production processes like lettering, there would be a need to either use more than one person at the printing workstation or to have more than one printing workstation. They could also develop simple stencils, thereby reducing the skills needed to do the job. If, on the other hand, you want to avoid a potential meltdown, then warn them of the risk. Provide some stencils of the lettering (see Section IV), let them subcontract out the lettering, do not require lettering of signs or loosen up how neatly or "legally" it must be done before the customer accepts it.

When producing complex products, like the basketball goal or road barrier, consider subcontracting out some of the more complex parts of the assemblies for corresponding price reduction. Of course, if you are playing a more advanced version, subcontracting, or simply not requiring lettering of signs, has already been mentioned. This same strategy can be considered for complex or extremely difficult production processes. For instance, the most complex product to make probably is the basketball backboard, rim, net, and post. The backboard, rim, and post are relatively easy, but the angles on the net are extremely difficult to do and stay within specifications. Therefore, consider allowing students the opportunity to either not make the net, or subcontract it out for price reductions.

The last product, the orange and white traffic drum, was designed entirely by students. In order to reduce the time that design engineering was taking up during a production run, students in an advanced version of the game were given the choice of coming up with some designs of their own. At this point the customer and producer would negotiate about price, quality standards and how many they could produce within the 30 minute period. In their version of the game, they had to show a 10 percent profit above their overhead. The customer agreed to pay 15 percent on any acceptable items the producer recommended.

At first, they were slow to suggest items. Then they were showed a toy drum and asked to come up with an acceptable design (one that would be tight enough to hold water). They developed the product, designed a new production process which involved wrapping construction paper around a metal end of a pipe, bending the bottom edge of the paper over and gluing a round circle to the bottom. Incidentally, the barrel did hold water! The student's budget vs. actual cost analysis is seen in Figure 9.

This process proved very successful. I suggest that you could ask for students to come up with designs for other gates, pallets, crates, or a variety of other items with the same good results.

BUDGET VS. ACTUAL
FOR BARRELS

	Budget	Actual	Variance
Total Materials	3200	4000	800 U
(estimated 8 sheets @ $400)			
Direct Labor	940	1160	220 U
(estimated 134 hours, about four workers)			
FOH:			
Indirect Labor	2450	2450	-0-
(salaries)			
Shipping Cost	400	200	200 F
(at least two shipments)			
Holding Cost FG	-0-	-0-	-0-
(none)			
Total Scrap	1700	1740	40 U
(85 inches of estimated scrap charged $20 per square inch)			
Scrap Disposal	85	87	2 U
(charged $1 if discarded)			
Warehouse Excess	372	372	-0-
(cost to carry inventory)			
(present inventory cost)			
Total Factory Overhead	5007	5669	662 U
COGM (Cost Of Goods Manufactured)	9147	10009	862 U

INCOME STATEMENT
BARRELS

	Budget	Actual	Variance
Sales	11250	9600	1650 U
(estimated 15 @ $750 sold 16 @ $600)			
COGM	9500	10009	509 U
(budget is from above plus an allowance)			
NI	1750	(409)	2159 U

Note: the unexpected sale of the stop signs brought the total sales to $18,600 and total expenses to $11,934. The stop signs were not budgeted.

Figure 9

ENGINEERING AND PRODUCTION SPECIFICATIONS

Product Request

Triangles 2 1/2 " x 2 1/2 " x 2 1/2 "

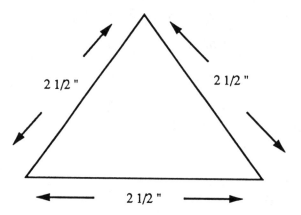

2 1/2 "   2 1/2 "

2 1/2 "

| Name: Brokerage House |
| Part: Triangles |
| Amount Needed: |
| Due Date: |
| Special Notes: |
| |
| |

ENGINEERING AND PRODUCTION SPECIFICATIONS

Product Request

Triangles 2 1/2 " x 2 1/2 " x 2 1/2 " at a price of $250.00.

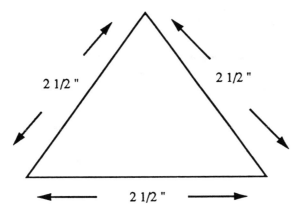

Name: Brokerage House	
Part: Triangles	
Amount Needed:	
Due Date:	
Special Notes:	

ENGINEERING AND PRODUCTION SPECIFICATIONS

Product Request

2 1/2 " x 1/2 " x 2 1/2 " x 4 " hour glass decorations (see diagram).
Need complete set of 8 or will not accept delivery.

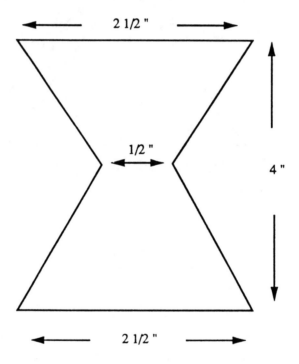

Name: Brokerage House	
Part: Hour glass decorations	
Amount Needed:	
Due Date:	
Special Notes: Hour glass must be in yellow or gold paper.	

ENGINEERING AND PRODUCTION SPECIFICATIONS

Product Request

2 1/2 " x 1/2 " x 2 1/2 " x 4 " hour glass decorations (see diagram) at a price of $350.00 per item. Need complete set of 8 or will not accept delivery.

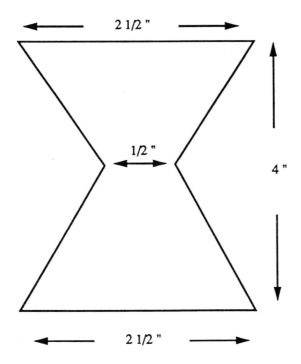

Name:	Brokerage House
Part:	Hour glass decorations
Amount Needed:	
Due Date:	
Special Notes:	Hour glass must be in yellow or gold paper.

ENGINEERING AND PRODUCTION SPECIFICATIONS
Product Request

I-Shaped pieces (see diagram).

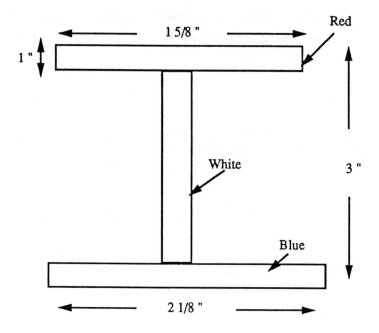

Name:	Brokerage House, Inc.
Part:	I-Brace
Amount Needed:	
Due Date:	
Special Notes: Each section of the I-shapes must	
be a different color. All widths should be 1".	

ENGINEERING AND PRODUCTION SPECIFICATIONS
Product Request

I-Shaped pieces (see diagram) at a price of $250.

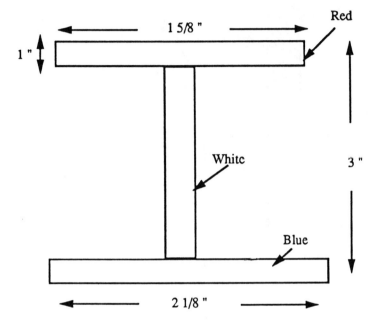

Name:	Brokerage House, Inc.
Part:	I-Brace
Amount Needed:	
Due Date:	
Special Notes:	Each section of the I-shapes must be a different color. All widths should be 1".

ENGINEERING AND PRODUCTION SPECIFICATIONS
Product Request

25 T- shaped pieces

3 "

1 1/2 "

1 "

1/2 "

4 1/2 "

1/2 "

2 "

Name:	Brokerage House
Part:	T- shaped piece
Amount Needed:	
Due Date:	
Special Notes:	Two different colors

ENGINEERING AND PRODUCTION SPECIFICATIONS

Product Request

25 T- shaped pieces at a price of $200.

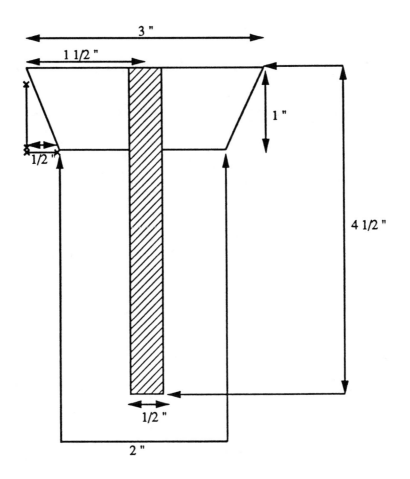

Name: Brokerage House	
Part: T- shaped piece	
Amount Needed:	
Due Date:	
Special Notes: Two different colors	

ENGINEERING AND PRODUCTION SPECIFICATIONS

Product Request

20 T-shaped pieces of 3" x 5" red and brown paper (see diagram)

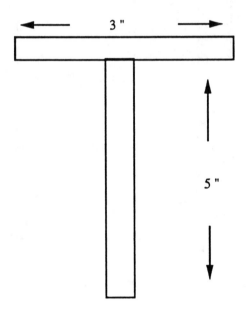

3 "

5 "

Name: Brokerage House
Part: T - brace
Amount Needed:
Due Date:
Special Notes: Need Exact Amount

ENGINEERING AND PRODUCTION SPECIFICATIONS

Product Request

20 T-shaped pieces of 3" x 5" red and brown paper (see diagram)
at a price of $150.

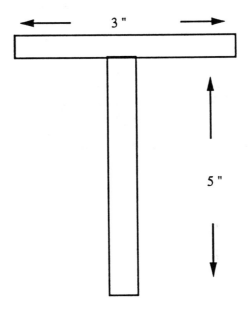

Name: Brokerage House	
Part: T - brace	
Amount Needed:	
Due Date:	
Special Notes: Need Exact Amount	

ENGINEERING AND PRODUCTION SPECIFICATIONS
Product Request

Four-link paper chains, each link a different color (link widths must be 3/4" and length of approximately 6" (see diagram). Must have 36.

Name: Brokerage House	
Part: Four-link paper chain	
Amount Needed:	
Due Date:	
Special Notes:	

ENGINEERING AND PRODUCTION SPECIFICATIONS
Product Request

Four-link paper chains, each link a different color (link widths must be 3/4" and length of approximately 6" (see diagram) at a price of $120.00. Must have 36.

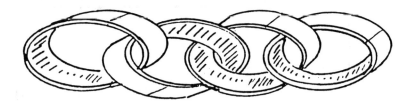

Name:	Brokerage House
Part:	Four-link paper chain
Amount Needed:	
Due Date:	
Special Notes:	

ENGINEERING AND PRODUCTION SPECIFICATIONS

Product Request

2 1/2 " x 3 1/2 " rectangle flags of any three colors.

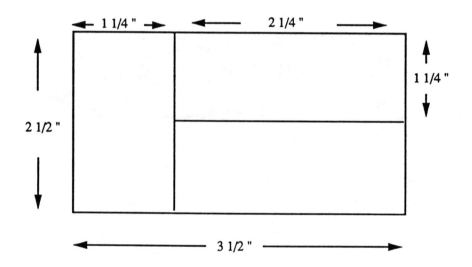

Name: Brokerage House	
Part: Rectangle Flags	
Amount Needed:	
Due Date:	
Special Notes: Must have prototype	

ENGINEERING AND PRODUCTION SPECIFICATIONS

Product Request

2 1/2 " x 3 1/2 " rectangle flags of any three colors at a price of $200.00 each.

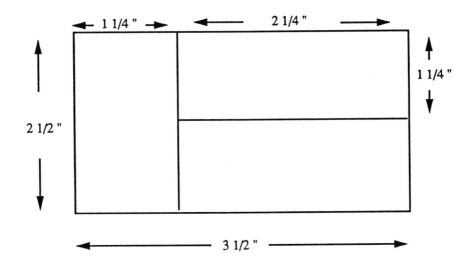

Name: Brokerage House	
Part: Rectangle Flags	
Amount Needed:	
Due Date:	
Special Notes: Must have prototype	

ENGINEERING AND PRODUCTION SPECIFICATIONS

Product Request

3 " x 3 " squares, 20 of those in purple color and 10 in gold.
Must be shipped 2 to 1 ratio.

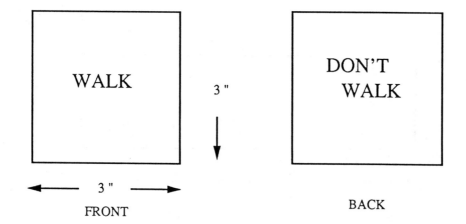

WALK   3 "   DON'T
                                               WALK

3 "

FRONT   BACK

Name:	Brokerage House
Part:	Walk/Don't Walk Sign
Amount Needed:	
Due Date:	
Special Notes:	

ENGINEERING AND PRODUCTION SPECIFICATIONS

Product Request

3 " x 3 " squares, 20 of those in purple color and 10 in gold at a price of $150.00.
Must be shipped 2 to 1 ratio.

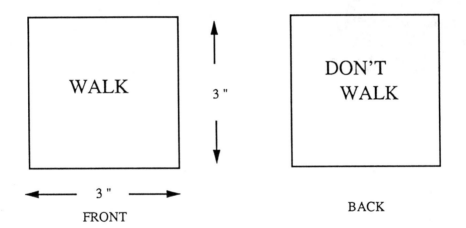

WALK	3 "		DON'T WALK

3 "

FRONT

BACK

Name:	Brokerage House
Part:	Walk/Don't Walk Sign
Amount Needed:	
Due Date:	
Special Notes:	

ENGINEERING AND PRODUCTION SPECIFICATIONS
Product Request

Problem-Solving Sign
2 1/2 " square

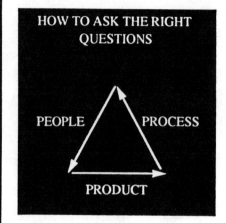

OR

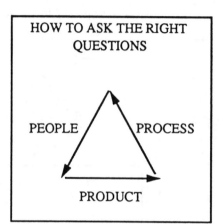

Name:	Brokerage House
Part:	Problem-Solving Sign
Amount Needed:	
Due Date:	
Special Notes:	

ENGINEERING AND PRODUCTION SPECIFICATIONS

Product Request

Sign at a price of $400 each.
2 1/2 " square

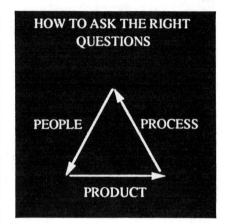

OR

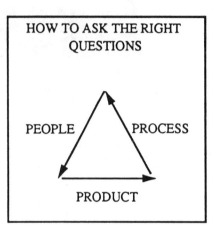

Name:	Brokerage House
Part:	Problem-Solving Sign
Amount Needed:	
Due Date:	
Special Notes:	

ENGINEERING AND PRODUCTION SPECIFICATIONS
Product Request

Red and blue warning sign

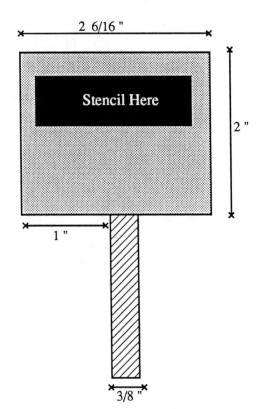

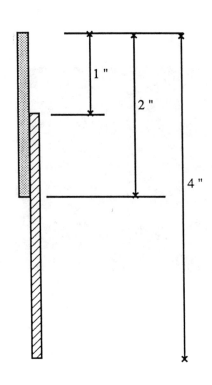

Name: Brokerage House	
Part: Red and Blue Warning Sign	
Amount Needed:	
Due Date:	
Special Notes:	

ENGINEERING AND PRODUCTION SPECIFICATIONS

Product Request

Red and blue warning sign at a price of $500.

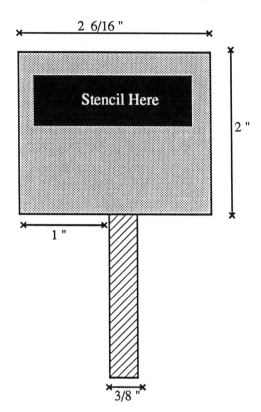

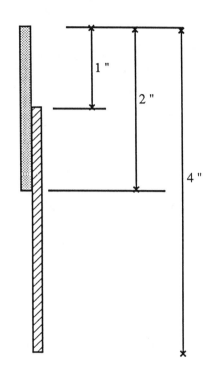

Name: Brokerage House

Part: Red and Blue Warning Sign

Amount Needed:

Due Date:

Special Notes:

ENGINEERING AND PRODUCTION SPECIFICATIONS
Product Request

Stop sign (see diagram) MUST HAVE DELIVERY WITHIN 20 MINUTES OF
PRODUCTION RUN. Must ship 10.

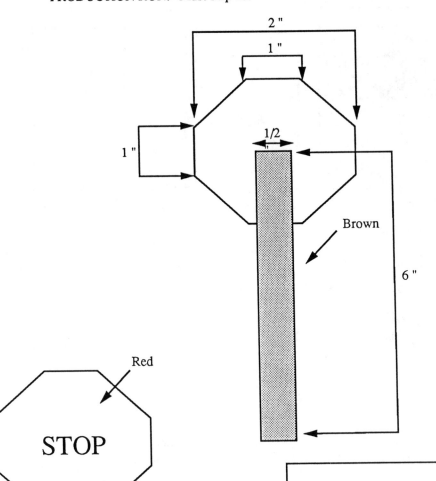

2 "

1 "

1 "

1/2 "

Brown

6 "

Red

STOP

Legal Letters, centered.
Black Lettering. Must
be neat!

Name: Brokerage House, Inc.	
Part: Stop sign	
Amount Needed:	
Due Date:	
Special Notes:	

ENGINEERING AND PRODUCTION SPECIFICATIONS
Product Request

Stop sign (see diagram) MUST HAVE DELIVERY WITHIN 20 MINUTES OF
PRODUCTION RUN. Price per sign, $1,150.00. Must ship 10.

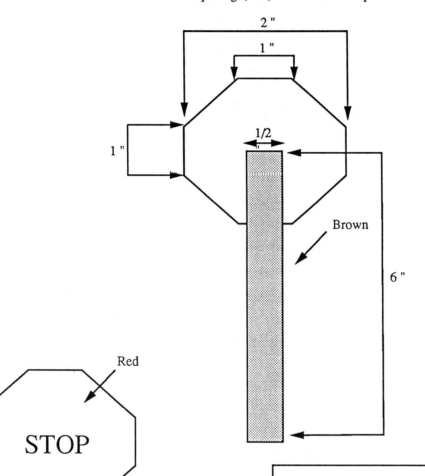

Red

STOP

Legal Letters, centered.
Black Lettering. Must
be neat!

Name: Brokerage House, Inc.	
Part: Stop sign	
Amount Needed:	
Due Date:	
Special Notes:	

ENGINEERING AND PRODUCTION SPECIFICATIONS

Product Request

20 yield signs (see specifications).

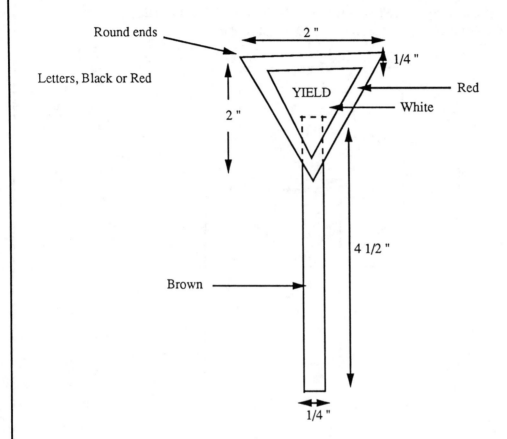

Round ends

Letters, Black or Red

2 "

2 "

1/4 "

YIELD

Red

White

4 1/2 "

Brown

1/4 "

Name:	Brokerage House
Part:	Yield sign
Amount Needed:	
Due Date:	
Special Notes:	

ENGINEERING AND PRODUCTION SPECIFICATIONS

Product Request

20 yield signs (see specifications) at a price of $900.00.

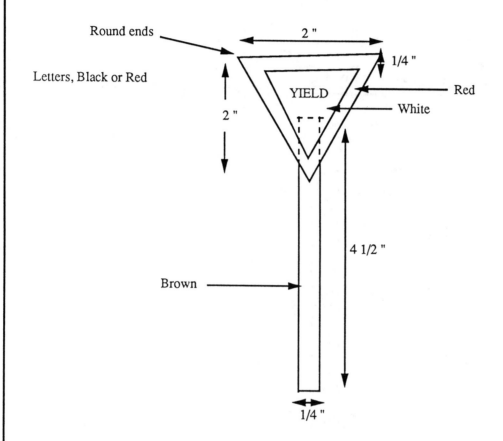

Round ends

Letters, Black or Red

2 "

2 "

1/4 "

YIELD

Red

White

4 1/2 "

Brown

1/4 "

Name:	Brokerage House
Part:	Yield sign
Amount Needed:	
Due Date:	
Special Notes:	

ENGINEERING AND PRODUCTION SPECIFICATIONS
Product Request

Route 66 gasoline signs (see diagram).   Need minimum of 10.

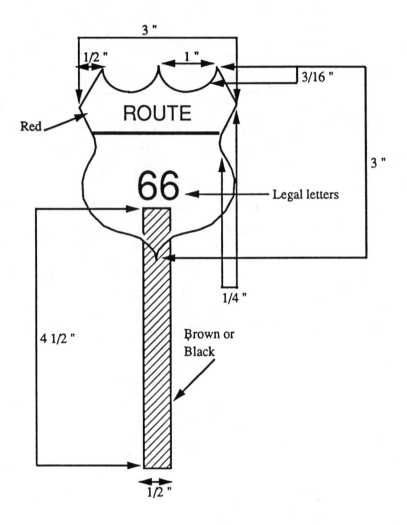

Name: Brokerage House

Part: Road sign

Amount Needed:

Due Date:

Special Notes:

ENGINEERING AND PRODUCTION SPECIFICATIONS

Product Request

Route 66 gasoline signs (see diagram) at a price of $1,350.00. Need minimum of 10.

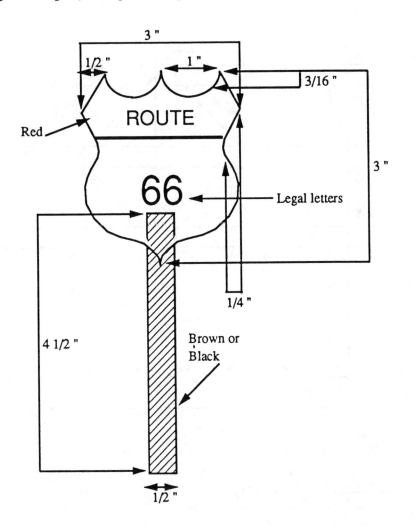

Name:	Brokerage House
Part:	Road sign
Amount Needed:	
Due Date:	
Special Notes:	

ENGINEERING AND PRODUCTION SPECIFICATIONS
Product Request

Road barrier (see diagram). Need 8 or will not accept lot.

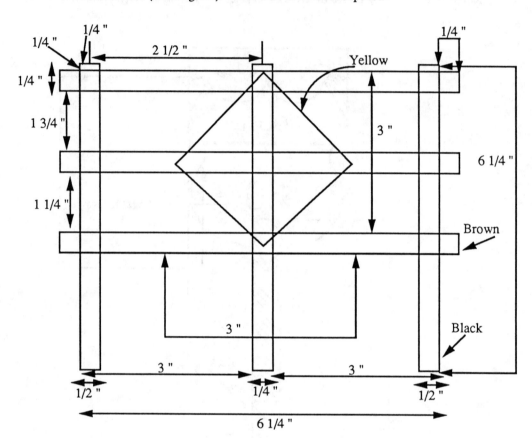

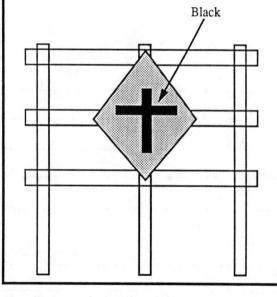

Black

| Name: Brokerage House, Inc. |
| Part: Road Barrier |
| Amount Needed: |
| Due Date: |
| Special Notes: |

ENGINEERING AND PRODUCTION SPECIFICATIONS
Product Request

Road barrier (see diagram) at a price of $1,650.00. Need 8 or will not accept lot.

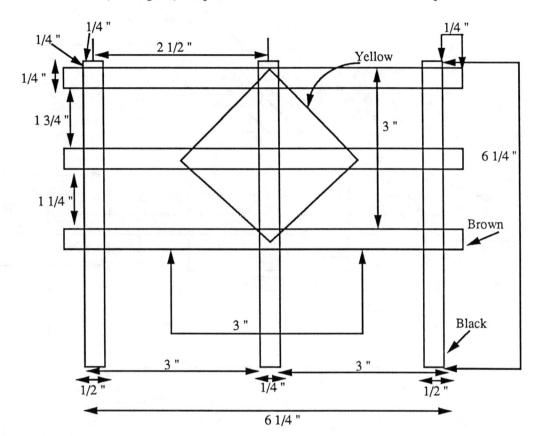

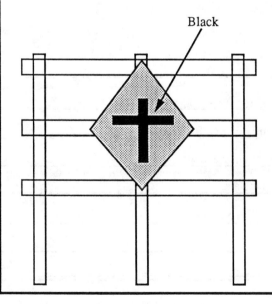

Black

Name: Brokerage House, Inc.

Part: Road Barrier

Amount Needed:

Due Date:

Special Notes:

ENGINEERING AND PRODUCTION SPECIFICATIONS
Product Request

Bridge barrier (see diagram). Need a minimum of 12 barriers.

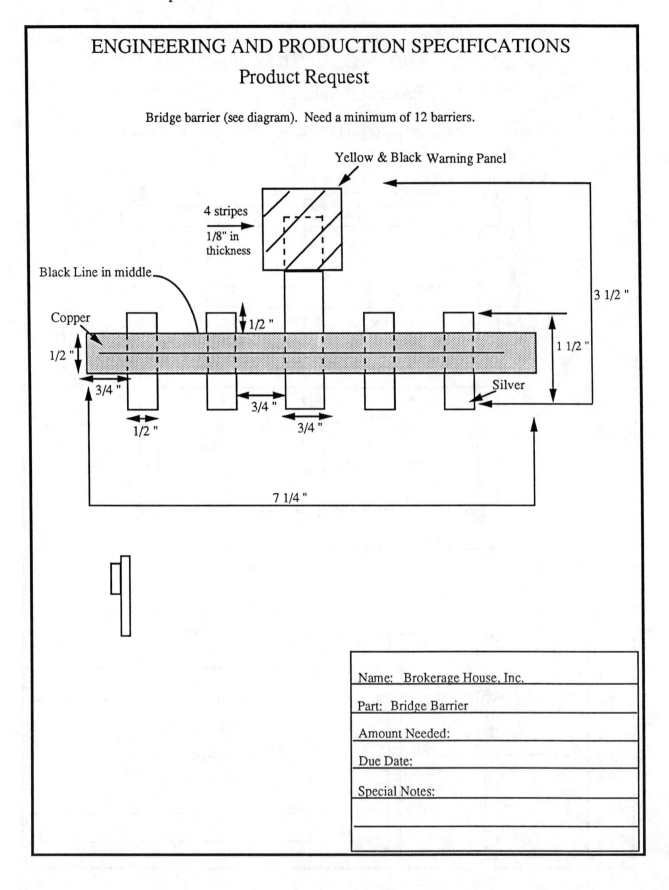

Name: Brokerage House, Inc.

Part: Bridge Barrier

Amount Needed:

Due Date:

Special Notes:

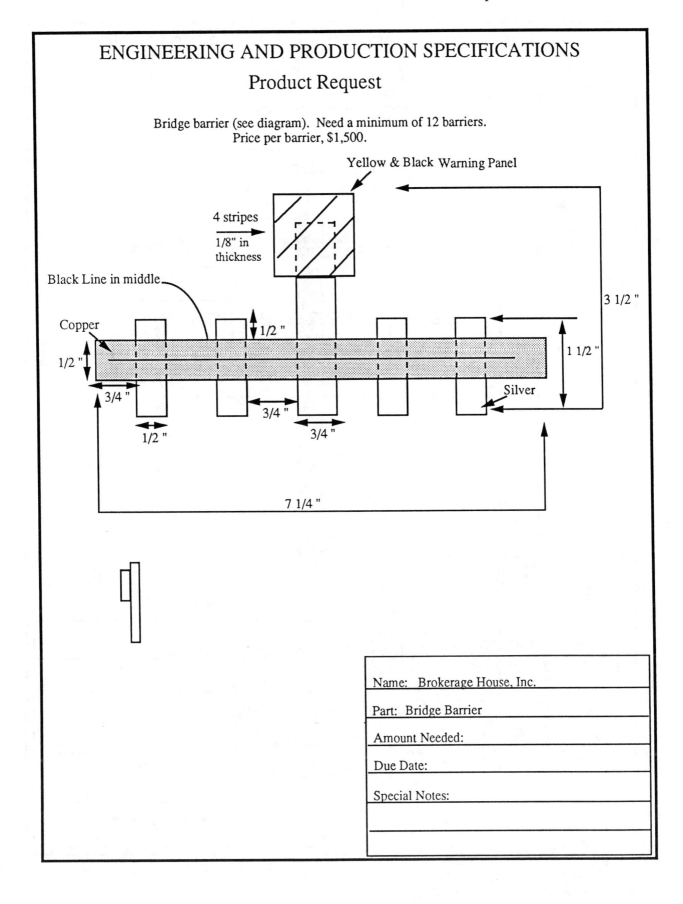

ENGINEERING AND PRODUCTION SPECIFICATIONS
Product Request

Bridge barrier (see diagram). Need a minimum of 12 barriers.
Price per barrier, $1,500.

Yellow & Black Warning Panel

4 stripes
1/8" in thickness

Black Line in middle

Copper

1/2 "

3/4 "

1/2 "

1/2 "

3/4 "

3/4 "

3 1/2 "

1 1/2 "

Silver

7 1/4 "

Name: Brokerage House, Inc.

Part: Bridge Barrier

Amount Needed:

Due Date:

Special Notes:

ENGINEERING AND PRODUCTION SPECIFICATIONS
Product Request

Three-way road sign (see diagram).

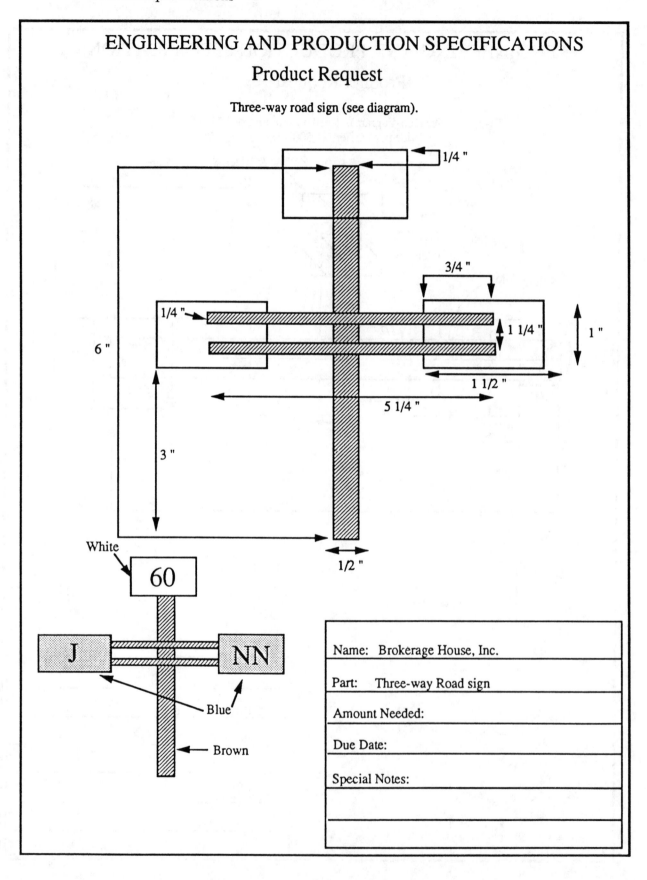

Name: Brokerage House, Inc.	
Part: Three-way Road sign	
Amount Needed:	
Due Date:	
Special Notes:	

ENGINEERING AND PRODUCTION SPECIFICATIONS
Product Request

Three-way road sign (see diagram) at a price of $2,000.

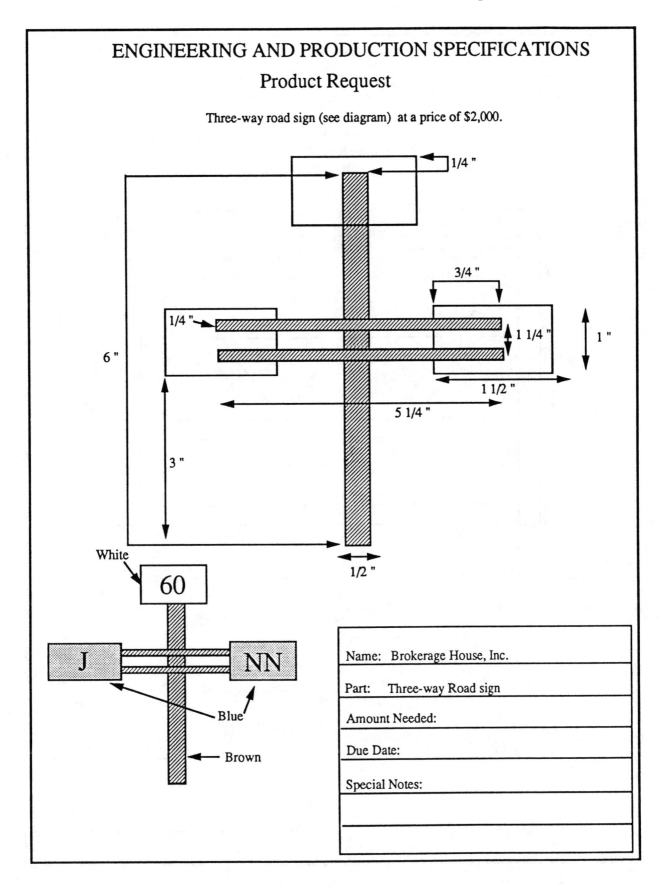

Name:	Brokerage House, Inc.
Part:	Three-way Road sign
Amount Needed:	
Due Date:	
Special Notes:	

ENGINEERING AND PRODUCTION SPECIFICATIONS

Product Request

Ranch gates (see specifications).   All planks are 1/4" unless otherwise noted. All in silver.
C NOBLE neatly lettered across front top of gate.
Rivet each plank.

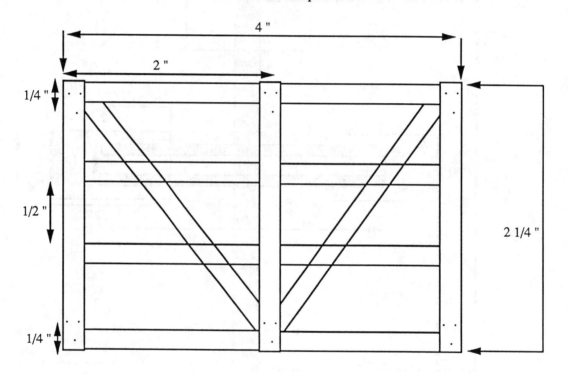

Name: Brokerage House
Part: Noble gate
Amount Needed:
Due Date:
Special Notes:

ENGINEERING AND PRODUCTION SPECIFICATIONS

Product Request

Ranch gates (see specifications) at a price of $650 per gate.   All planks are 1/4" unless otherwise noted. All in silver. C NOBLE neatly lettered across front top of gate. Rivet each plank.

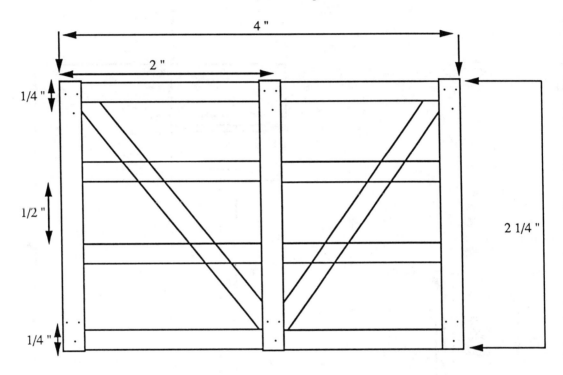

Name: Brokerage House
Part: Noble gate
Amount Needed:
Due Date:
Special Notes:

ENGINEERING AND PRODUCTION SPECIFICATIONS
Product Request

Basketball goal, backboard, post and net (see diagram).
Minimum order 8; maximum order 30.

2 "

1 "

1/8 "

1 "

6 1/8 "

White

Orange

3/8 "

Black

1/2 "

Name:	Brokerage House, Inc.
Part:	Basketball goal
Amount Needed:	
Due Date:	
Special Notes:	

ENGINEERING AND PRODUCTION SPECIFICATIONS
Product Request

Basketball goal, backboard, post and net (see diagram) at a price of $1,700.00.
Minimum order 8; maximum order 30.

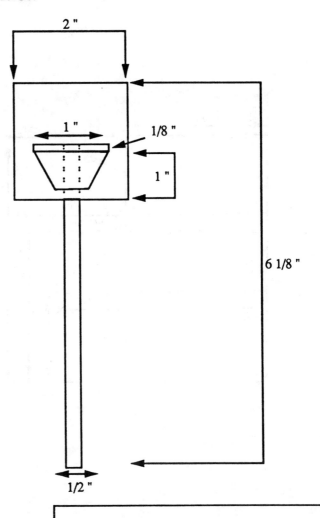

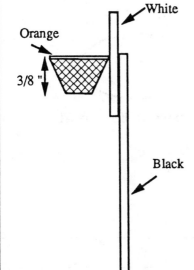

Name: Brokerage House, Inc.	
Part: Basketball goal	
Amount Needed:	
Due Date:	
Special Notes:	

ENGINEERING AND PRODUCTION SPECIFICATIONS
Product Request

Traffic Safety Drum

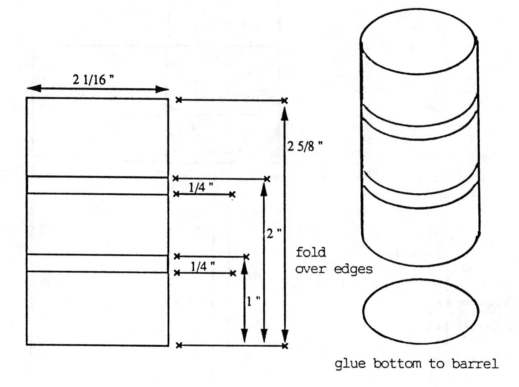

2 1/16 "

2 5/8 "

1/4 "

2 "

1/4 "

1 "

fold
over edges

glue bottom to barrel

Name: Brokerage House	
Part: Traffic Safety Drum	
Amount Needed:	
Due Date:	
Special Notes: Orange with white stripes;	
Closed bottom, open top.	

ENGINEERING AND PRODUCTION SPECIFICATIONS
Product Request

Name: Brokerage House	
Part:	
Amount Needed:	
Due Date:	
Special Notes:	

ENGINEERING AND PRODUCTION SPECIFICATIONS
Product Request

Name: Brokerage House

Part:

Amount Needed:

Due Date:

Special Notes:

ENGINEERING AND PRODUCTION SPECIFICATIONS
Product Request

Name: Brokerage House

Part:

Amount Needed:

Due Date:

Special Notes:

ENGINEERING AND PRODUCTION SPECIFICATIONS
Product Request

Name: Brokerage House	
Part:	
Amount Needed:	
Due Date:	
Special Notes:	

ENGINEERING AND PRODUCTION SPECIFICATIONS
Product Request

Name: Brokerage House	
Part:	
Amount Needed:	
Due Date:	
Special Notes:	

SECTION III

SUPPLEMENTAL PRODUCTION MATERIALS
AND FORMS

Materials contained in the final two sections of the manual can be used to enhance various aspects of the simulation. The stencil sheets, shown after the Index in Section IV, are one such example.

As previously noted, the printing of signs is one of the more difficult and time-consuming processes. Often, as in running advanced versions, it is good for students to face this challenge. Sometimes, however, you may want to make it easier on the management team or you may simply want to have them produce as many products as possible. If so, you might want to reduce the amount of writing the students do by using the stenciling shortcut. Stenciling is also something that the students' supplier, Muscleman, could sell to them.

The first part of Section III has three examples of consultant reports that were provided to the management teams. Each report is based on the comments of an outside CEO, Plant Manager, Inventory or Production Manager, or other top officials of local industries. They were asked to watch the production run by the students and comment, immediately after the run, about what they liked and what needed improvement. They were asked to briefly write down their comments, which were later typed, except for example number three. This consultant typed up his own letter and presented a detailed analysis to the company's CEO. This report provides the best example of the information that can be contained in these reports.

Each of the guest speaker's or consultant's comments were also videotaped so the management team could review it, along with the typed consultant's report, if they needed more information. The consultant report was the main piece of information, along with the forms and measurements students themselves were tracking, that was used in the students manager's meetings. These production forms and measurements are shown in the next section of this manual and are included in every student's Study Guide.

The second part of this section on Supplemental Production Materials provides an example of the Stockholders' Report that was used in one of the advanced versions of the simulation. These reports were to be prepared by the CEO, with help from his/her management team. They were to be typed up after each management meeting and were to summarize what changes were to be made before the next production run.

Pages two and three of the report summarized material cost, direct labor and factory overhead cost for the previous production run. The report also contained net income, overhead percentages, and gross income margin for the company.

The last page of the report showed a graph of the percentages. (Since the students' evaluation was based largely on their reports of lowering overhead, this discussion was the central theme of their management meeting.) A blank Stockholders' Report is also provided, although each instructor may wish to create his/her own report emphasizing the areas in which he or she has the most interest.

The last part of Section IV is the money that can be used when using a more advanced version that emphasizes profitability as well as productivity. The cash is used by the management team to purchase material and equipment from their supplier, Muscleman. It is also used by their customer, the Brokerage House, to pay for the goods that the students sell. Remember, employees get $7 an hour or whatever pay system management develops.

Admittedly, cash is not needed to run the simulations. It just makes the simulation more fun, just as does much of this supplemental material.

EXAMPLE OF

CONSULTANTS' REPORTS

DUFF CONSULTANT REPORT
(Example #1)

Problem

(1) Prototype (written) specifications not spelled out on parts.

(2) Production Manger should be part of design team.

Make lots in smaller amounts (e.g., instead of designing lot of 8 stop signs to a page, use lot of 2 stop signs per page). This gets people started working sooner.

(3) Production people in place before actually required.

(4)   Selection of product a problem--maybe too ambitious for size of factory.

(5)   Might consider setting up a process planner in the organization to interface between manufacturing and engineering (buys tools, equipment and selects processes).

Third production run

WILSON CONSULTANT REPORT
(Example #2)

STRONG POINTS

- went back to customer several times to clarify design
- made "first piece" check (will) make sure it meets spec's
- good pieces being produced, everybody took task at hand
- were aggressive, went for the "GOLD"

OBSERVATIONS & IMPROVEMENTS

-improved productivity but shipped some defective product (Q. C. & shipping agreed to ship it)

-engineering efficiency improved but some questionable designs (T-shaped device: Why was flap folded added 30% to material cost but resulted in better quality--was it worth it?)

-was recommendation that manufacturing engineering (process engineer) might be needed to improve productivity (middle person between design engineers and production would have said "it can't be done that way and meet 1/16" specs' ")

-if changes made need written S.O.P.'s (all good companies have them) that go all the way back to make sure everyone knows change

-suggestion for a shop traveler that shows where product is at in production process, so won't run out of time and wind up with extra material

UPDATE MANUFACTURING LAYOUT   (design, manufacturing, and Q.C. at
end of line resembles 1900's)

-recommendation was made to set up in-process inspection (or SPC) would identify quicker that "something is wrong" (either bad design or inappropriate tooling)

-use die cutting (one stroke to cut several pieces)

-use templates (ask engineering for them--lay piece on it, to see if it's a good one) as alternative to reading ruler

-ask customer for two or three sets of spec's so production people can be studying them (use them as Q.C. circle--design production environment while engineer design product)

-would know "by golly" can't make 8 folds and expect to be within 1/16"

-When I get a customer who says I want it to "look nice" make one, give it to customer, if they like it, keep it, so will not have questions later.

-When rework decide if material and labor outweigh value of redoing it.

-shipping and receiving need to keep track of how many are shipped.

-responsible for everything up and down stream from you.

-everybody should question everybody (flip of coin)

CONSULTANTS REPORT
(Example # 3)

Noble Manufacturing Company
SMSU, Springfield, MO
ATTN: Mr. Jeff Pelts
    Chief Executive Officer

Dear Mr. Pelts:

After observing the start-up activities of Noble Manufacturing Company per your request I have
documented my comments hoping to assist you in improving your operation. Below are my constructive
and commending comments:

ORGANIZATION:

You should re-evaluate your organizational structure for two purposes.

1.   Areas of responsibility relative to the number of staff members available and
where you need to put your emphasis of control. Reassess your resources
relative to your requirements.

I think that you should be placing more attention especially in the start-up phase,
more in the area of production management.

You can accomplish this with some combining of responsibilities, such as
purchasing, inventory, and warehousing under one person to free up people for
positions closer to the primary function of production.

2.   Assignment of your personnel to the various management positions relative to
their aptitudes, interests, training, and education. Example, the warehouse
manager developed a template for inspecting the product on the production line.

Maybe this person should be in Engineering developing product designs,
specifications, manufacturing processes, and tooling, or Production, or QC.

Another suggestion is to have your Human Resources Manager conducting the
training of production workers in the basic production methods of cutting,
trimming and gluing; prior to the start of production.

PLANNING:

There are some key people that should be present for their inputs as the Engineering Department develops the specs, processes, work station layouts, and tooling requirements. But don't "crowd" up the area.

These are in addition to engineering:
1. Production
2. Purchasing/Inventory/Warehouse
3. Production Training (Human Resources)
4. Quality Control
5. Marketing

Once the specs are prepared then each department head can determine their needs and set out to fill them.

PROCEDURE:

1. Customers' orders to Marketing for complete review of product-
   Description
   Complete specs, color, dimensions, etc. (call customer if unclear--don't guess)
   Quantity
   Delivery--Partial shipments, complete order, packaging, etc.
   Quality requirements--areas that are critical, major or minor

2. Marketing turns order with spec sheets to Engineering.
   Engineering reviews specs with Marketing.
   Engineering determines material requirements, production methods and production process, facilities, tooling, inspection requirements and manpower requirements.
   Engineering then reviews the above items with the management "team."

WORK ASSIGNMENT:

- Purchasing/Inventory/Warehouse - secures materials as Engineering specifies, stores and issues to Production.
  Receives finished product from Production, stores and ships to customer.

- Human Resources--secures hourly workforce personnel, trains in basic production methods of cutting, trimming, and gluing. Assists production supervision at production start-up.

- Quality Control--works with Engineering regarding quality specs, testing and inspection methods. Construct or have constructed testing and inspection fixtures as required to guarantee required customer quality levels.

Keeps production management informed of any specific or quality trends.

Responsible for keeping defective materials separated from acceptable products.

- Production Management--
    - Insures hourly workforce is trained.
    - Sets up production operation according to Engineering direction (secures tools, tables, etc.)
    - Instructs and supervises the hourly workforce in the production function--following engineering processes--maybe add supervision using hourly people as group leaders or pull supervision from other management areas through consolidation.
    - Constant monitoring of production operation for improvement in flow, operator performance, etc.

- Engineering--
    - Spec. Review
    - Material requirements--per unit
    - Production methods, process, facilities, tooling, staffing, and inspection requirements

- Marketing--
    - Sales
    - Customer contact and relations
    - Spec. requirements

- Finance--
    - Payment of bills
    - Cost collection
    - Cost review with C.E.O. and other key management team members.

OBSERVATIONS:

Negative:

1. Too many people involved in initial customer order review.
2. Incomplete specs from customer, accepted by Engineering with assumptions made. A sample would have been good.
3. Purchasing Department was told to secure material even before the requirements (amount or configuration) were determined.
4. Engineering did not determine the manpower, equipment, or process requirements.
5. The C.E.O. became the complete management team in one person, starting with engineering, production, inspection, etc.
6. The Quality Control Manager did not develop his staff and set up positions, testing and inspection fixtures, etc.--the Warehouse Manager developed an inspection fixture.
7. The Production Manager did not lay out his production facility and supervise the workforce because the C.E.O. took over.
8. There was no pre-training of the production workforce in the basic production tasks of cutting, trimming, and gluing.

9. A one or two piece pilot run could have been run prior to commitment to starting production to "debug" and locate potential problems.

10. There was no control of the hourly workforce. They should be kept in one area away from the operation until needed. This time could have been used for the production training. This was contributing to the chaos.

11. A layout of the complete operation to enhance the flow of information, materials support to the production line and removal of finished product from the production line to the finished goods storage.
It was very congested in the whole area and there was no defined channel of communications as to production data, quality data, etc.

12. Overall, there was a general lack of organization and, as a result, there was a lot of chaos. Organization enhances communications, productivity, good quality, and all those other things that make for success.

13. Do more inspection early in the process, especially at the start of a new product--then reduced inspection.

Positive:

1. The Engineering Department did their experimenting using non-productive materials which is a savings.

2. The Engineering Department did a good job of laying out the product to the materials which conserved the use of productive materials by reducing the material usage requirements.

3. The Human Resource Department had workers available and on time.

4. There was a tremendous spirit of working together on the part of both the management and hourly personnel. It needs to be better directed.

5. Some of the management team members showed they had some experience and they utilized it as shown by some of the actions they took.

6. Some acceptable product was turned out.

OVERALL:

The operation was not a "melt down" and with more definitive organization responsibilities and better utilization of the management and hourly workforce, you will see great improvement. You should spend your time observing the operation rather than direct involvement.

At the end of each day sit down with your management team and review what happened to the operations--results, problems, etc. and solicit them for suggestions for improvement for the next day. Don't come in the next day expecting the same problems you had today. Make improvements.

You should ask your Engineering Department about some production methods improvements. How about some semi-automation such as the use of paper cutters so you can cut several sheets at the same time. (Keep safety requirements in mind--no missing fingers.)

Set up a separate operation for making components and feed the final assembly line.

Keep the work content as simple and short as possible so that you take advantage of the benefits of specialization. Also, when an experienced operator is absent or you have a new work position, the training requirements and learning curves are reduced.

May these comments assist you in being more successful.

Respectfully submitted,

Tom Holt

EXAMPLE OF

STOCKHOLDERS' QUARTERLY REPORTS

QUARTERLY REPORT

MANUFACTURING
COMPANY

March 4,

From the desk of
to the stockholders of
        Manufacturing Company

Dear Fellow Stockholders:

The changes we implemented after our first production period proved to be very beneficial to our company. Generally, all departments operated better by being more effective at their specific tasks. We operated much more like an integrated team. However, in spite of our tremendous work effort, new problems arose, and consequently we have proposed additional changes to improve our productivity.

Again with the advice from outside consultants and internal managers, we have created a list of proposed changes. They are as follows:

1.   Train production workers better. It is critical that they be able to follow directions and do their assigned tasks.

2.   Test the employees to find out which skills they possess, such as cutting, layout, assembling, etc., and assign each of them to the task they excel in.

3.   Create an additional line supervisor to aid and assist the production manager. Eventually we may have to operate two separate production lines.

4.   Combine the Finance, Purchasing, Warehousing, and Shipping functions under one manager. This will enable us to use our staff more efficiently.

5.   The CEO, Production, and Finance will choose which products we will manufacture. By having these people in on the selection process we can better select the products that can be built cost effectively.

6.   Better utilize product specification sheets. Orient workers better as to what they will be building in the preproduction period.

MANUFACTURING COMPANY
STATEMENT OF COST OF GOODS (COGS) MANUFACTURED
For Production Period:

Current manufacturing costs:

    Cost of materials placed in production:

Stores control, beginning	1,600			
Purchases	1,900			
Total materials available	3,500			
Stores control, ending	800			
Total materials placed into production		2,700		
Direct labor 260 minutes x 7.00 hr.		1,820		

Factory overhead

Indirect labor	5 x 300.00	1,500	
Shipping costs	2 shipments x 200.00	400	
Holding cost FG			
Total cost Scrap	200 sq. inches x 200.00	4,000	
Total factory overhead		5,900	

COST OF GOODS MANUFACTURED   10,420

INCOME STATEMENT

Sales	9,300	
Cost of goods manufactured	10,420	
Gross profit		-1,120
Administrative expenses	950	
Equipment/Supplies	9,200	
NET INCOME		-11,270

MANUFACTURING COMPANY
Supplemental Summary Report
For Production Period:

The following percentages are derived by comparing separate costs to the total cost of goods manufactured:

Total materials placed into production.

$$\frac{\text{total materials placed into production}}{\text{COGM}} = -\frac{2,700}{10,420} = 25.9\%$$

Direct labor.

$$\frac{\text{direct labor}}{\text{COGM}} = \frac{1,820}{10,420} = 17.5\%$$

Total scrap cost.

$$\frac{\text{total scrap cost}}{\text{COGM}} = \frac{4,000}{10,420} = 38.4\%$$

Total factory overhead.

$$\frac{\text{total factory overhead}}{\text{COGM}} = \frac{5,900}{10,420} = 56.6\%$$

Gross income margin.

$$\frac{\text{gross profit}}{\text{sales}} = \frac{-1,120}{9,300} = -12.0\%$$

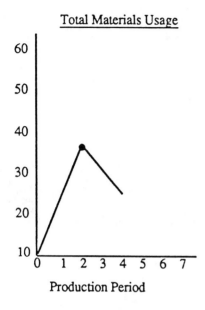

Total Materials Usage

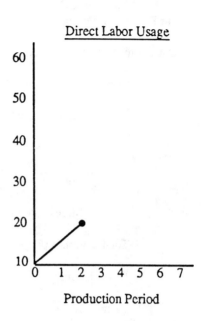

Direct Labor Usage

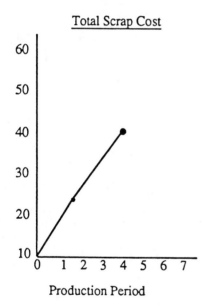

Total Scrap Cost

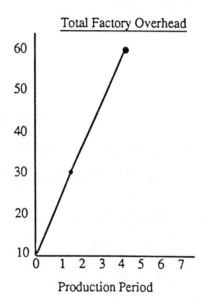

Total Factory Overhead

MANUFACTURING COMPANY
STATEMENT OF COST OF GOODS (COGS) MANUFACTURED
For Production Period:_____

Current manufacturing costs:

    Cost of materials placed in production:

        Stores control, beginning

        Purchases

        Total materials available

        Stores control, ending

    Total materials placed into production

    Direct labor

    Factory overhead

        Indirect labor

        Shipping costs

        Holding cost FG

        Total cost Scrap

    Total factory overhead

COST OF GOODS MANUFACTURED

INCOME STATEMENT

Sales

Cost of goods manufactured

Gross profit

Administrative expenses

Equipment/Supplies

NET INCOME

MANUFACTURING COMPANY
Supplemental Summary Report
For Production Period:

_____

The following percentages are derived by comparing separate costs to the total cost of goods manufactured:

Total materials placed into production.

$$\frac{\text{total materials placed into production}}{\text{COGM}} = \_$$

Direct labor.

$$\frac{\text{direct labor}}{\text{COGM}} =$$

Total scrap cost.

$$\frac{\text{total scrap cost}}{\text{COGM}} =$$

Total factory overhead.

$$\frac{\text{total factory overhead}}{\text{COGM}} =$$

Gross income margin.

$$\frac{\text{gross profit}}{\text{sales}} =$$

Total Materials Usage

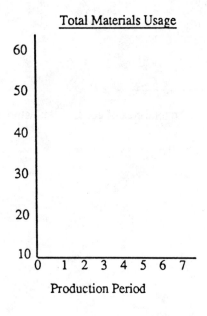

Production Period

Direct Labor Usage

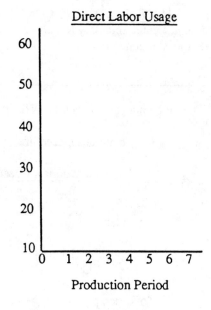

Production Period

Total Scrap Cost

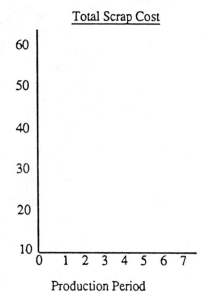

Production Period

Total Factory Overhead

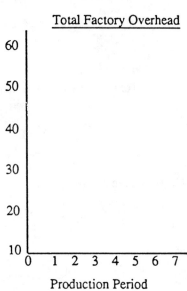

Production Period

SECTION IV

FOR TEACHER'S EYES ONLY

Not everyone who uses this simulation is a teacher. Some users are consultants while others are corporate trainers. A teacher's perspective is different because part of his or her responsibility is to evaluate performance and then come up with some form of assignment of grades.

This last section of the manual contains some examples of instructions to students on how to play the game. These instructions, or similar ones, can be used to supplement those directions that the students have in their Study Guide. The instructions in the guide tell students how to play the game, how to do well at it, and provide the necessary forms. The instructions in this manual supplement this by showing examples of how students can be graded for both the basic and advanced versions of the game.

Instructions for the basic option include descriptions of various organizational aspects including what happens if the students' products are rejected upon inspection. The grading and scoring section of these instructions notes the responsibility of the student CEO in running the company.

These instructions were designed for students who were to make four production runs during a semester. Therefore, the third page of these instructions describes how they will be graded for each production run. As seen in the instructions, students were only evaluated on their productivity in the first production run. The second, third and fourth production runs successively consider inventory, quality and labor utilization. The grade sheet also summarizes the total points available for participating in the simulation. In the first grade sheet (Figure 10) there are eight teams (one large lecture hall of 110 students). The grade sheet immediately behind this grade sheet (Figure 11) was produced when I used the game in three different classes and had a total of sixteen teams competing with each other.

One final way of evaluating students, using the basic option, is seen in the third grading example Figure 12). This particular grading sheet classified the criteria in three categories: productivity, quality

FIRST EXAMPLE OF

GRADING FOR PRODUCTION GAME

1st Production Run

Criteria	1st	2nd	3rd	4th	5th	6th	7th	8th
Points received	7.0	6.3	6.1	5.8	5.6	5.4	5.2	4.9
%	100%	90%	87%	83%	80%	77%	74.5%	70%

2nd Production Run

Criteria	1st	2nd	3rd	4th	5th	6th	7th	8th
Units produced	8.0	7.0	7.0	6.7	6.5	6.3	6.1	5.7
Inventory	2.0	2.0	1.8	1.8	1.5	1.5	1.3	1.3
Total pts.	10.0	9.0	8.8	8.5	8.0	7.8	7.4	7.0
%	100%	90%	88%	85%	80%	78%	74%	70%

3rd Production Run

Criteria	1st	2nd	3rd	4th	5th	6th	7th	8th
Units produced	8.0	7.0	7.0	6.6	6.6	6.4	6.2	5.9
Inventory	2.5	2.5	2.2	2.2	1.9	1.8	1.7	1.6
Scrap, rework	2.5	2.5	2.2	2.2	1.9	1.8	1.7	1.6
Total pts.	13.0	12.0	11.4	11.0	10.4	10.0	9.6	9.1
%	100%	92%	88%	85%	80%	77%	74%	70%

4th Production Run

Criteria	1st	2nd	3rd	4th	5th	6th	7th	8th
Units produced	8.0	7.0	7.0	6.5	6.5	6.0	6.0	5.5
Inventory	2.5	2.5	2.1	2.1	1.9	1.8	1.7	1.7
Quality	2.5	2.5	2.1	2.1	1.9	1.8	1.7	1.7
Labor Utilization	2.0	2.0	2.0	1.9	1.9	1.8	1.7	1.7
Total pts.	15.0	14.0	13.2	12.6	12.2	11.4	11.1	10.5
%	100%	94%	88%	84%	81.5%	76%	74%	70%

Figure 10

SECOND EXAMPLE OF

GRADING FOR PRODUCTION GAME

1st Production Run

Criteria	1st	2nd	3rd	4th	5th	6th	7th	8th	9th	10th	11th	12th	13th	14th	15th	16th
Points received	7.0	6.8	6.6	6.3	6.1	6.0	5.8	5.6	5.5	5.3	5.1	4.9	4.8	4.7	4.6	4.5
%	100%	97%	94%	90%	87%	85%	83%	80%	78.5%	75.7	72.9	70%	68.6%	67%	65.7%	64%

2nd Production Run

Criteria	1st	2nd	3rd	4th	5th	6th	7th	8th	9th	10th	11th	12th	13th	14th	15th	16th
Units produced	8.0	7.8	7.5	7.2	7.0	6.8	6.6	6.4	6.2	6.0	5.8	5.6	5.4	5.3	5.2	5.0
Inventory	2.0	1.9	1.9	1.3	1.7	1.7	1.6	1.6	1.5	1.5	1.4	1.4	1.4	1.3	1.3	1.2
Total Pts.	10.0	9.7	9.4	9.0	8.7	8.5	8.2	3.0	7.7	7.5	7.2	7.0	2.8	2.2	2.5	6.2
%	100%	97%	94%	90%	87%	85%	82%	80%	77%	75%	72%	70%	68%	66%	65%	62%

3rd Production Run

Criteria	1st	2nd	3rd	4th	5th	6th	7th	8th	9th	10th	11th	12th	13th	14th	15th	16th
Units produced	8.0	7.7	7.5	7.2	7.0	6.8	6.6	6.4	6.2	6.0	5.8	5.6	5.4	5.3	5.2	5.0
Inventory	2.5	2.5	2.4	2.3	2.2	2.1	2.1	2.0	2.0	1.9	1.8	1.7	1.7	1.6	1.5	1.5
Scrap, rework	2.5	2.4	2.4	2.3	2.2	2.1	2.0	2.0	1.9	1.9	1.8	1.7	1.7	1.6	1.5	1.4
Total Pts.	13.0	12.6	12.3	11.8	11.4	11.0	10.7	10.4	10.1	9.8	9.4	9.1	8.3	8.5	8.2	7.9
%	100%	97.0%	94.6%	90.7%	87.7%	84.6%	82.3%	80%	77.7%	75.9%	72.3%	70%	67.7%	65%	63%	61%

4th Production Run

Criteria	1st	2nd	3rd	4th	5th	6th	7th	8th	9th	10th	11th	12th	13th	14th	15th	16th
Units produced	8.0	7.8	7.6	7.3	7.1	6.8	6.7	6.6	6.6	6.5	6.3	6.3	6.3	6.1	6.0	5.8
Inventory	2.5	2.5	2.4	2.3	2.2	2.2	2.1	2.0	1.9	1.8	1.7	1.6	1.5	1.4	1.3	1.3
Quality	2.5	2.4	2.3	2.2	2.1	2.1	2.0	1.9	1.8	1.7	1.6	1.5	1.4	1.3	1.2	1.2
Labor Utilization	2.0	1.9	1.8	1.7	1.6	1.6	1.5	1.5	1.4	1.3	1.2	1.1	1.0	1.0	1.0	1.0
Total pts.	15.0	14.6	14.1	13.5	13.0	12.7	12.3	12.0	11.7	11.3	10.8	10.5	10.2	9.8	9.5	9.3
%	100%	97.3%	94%	90%	86.7%	84.7%	82%	80%	78%	75.3%	72%	70%	68%	65%	63.3%	62%

Figure 11

THIRD EXAMPLE OF

GRADING FOR BASIC PRODUCTION

CRITERIA	1st	2nd	3rd	4th	5th	6th	7th	8th
Productivity	7.0	6.0	6.0	5.0	5.0	5.0	4.5	4.5
Scrap, Rework and Work-in-Process	2.0	2.0	1.8	1.8	1.7	1.5	1.3	1.3
Raw Material and Finished Goods (not shipped)	2.0	2.0	1.6	1.6	1.5	1.5	1.2	1.2
Total Points	11	10	9 .4	8.4	8.2	8.0	7.0	7.0

100% = 11
90% = 9.9
85% = 9.35
80% = 8.8
75% = 8.25
70% = 7.7
65% = 7.15

A = 85% or above
B = 75% or above
C = 65% or above

Figure 12

(scrap, rework) and inventory (raw materials, finished goods). This classroom also had eight rows, so all the numbers were set up to evaluate eight companies that ranged from A to G.

The sheet immediately behind this example (Figure 13) shows that these companies were ranked against each other on several variables including how many lots or batches of products they were able to produce in a 30 minute production run. For instance, Company A produced five lots (each lot contained four items). They finished third in this category and received 6 points for their effort. They had 264 square inches of scrap, rework and other extra inventory after their production runs. This placed Company A seventh in this category and they received 2-1/2 points. These points, along with their 6 points for finishing third in production, resulted in 8-1/2 (or 77 percent) out of a maximum of eleven (11) possible points.

In an interesting twist, all materials were purchased from the instructor at a cost of $25 an inch and they sold their products for $100 each. This created a crude relative measure, seen in Figure 14, of each company's profit or loss during the production run. For instance, since Company A had 264 square inches of excess material, they had a material cost of $6,600 (264 x $25.00 = $6,600).

The fourth example includes the Directions for THE PRODUCTION GAME - advanced version of the game. Grading for the game is based on "meeting the customer's expectations." In this game, the student's job shop company was referred to as Noble Manufacturing Company.

These instructions, as well as information in the Study Guide, remind participants to organize their company around functional departments (finance, quality control, etc.) and to focus on cycle time. Cycle time is a good measure to judge performance since one must "do it right the first time" in order to produce a product with any speed. Rework and repair are signs of poor organization and will slow down the organization.

The directions for the advanced version remind students that they can purchase materials from their supplier, Muscleman, and the necessity of keeping detailed and up-to-date records of output, labor utilization and other relevant measures. The instructions also remind students how much raw materials will cost them, as well as transportation costs and income available at the start of the game.

Comparison of companies based on productivity, excessive scrap, rework and excess inventory

Company	Production	Placement	Points	Materials Scrap Rework	Placement	Points	Grade
A	5	3rd	6	264	7th	2.5	8.5=77%
B	4	4th	5	176	6th	3.0	8.0=73%
C	6	2nd	6	40	2nd	4	10.0=91%
D	6	3rd	6	78	4th	3.4	9.2=84%
E	5	3rd	6	110	5th	3.2	9.2=84%
F	*10	1st	7	56	3rd	3.4	10.4=95%
G	* 2	5th	5	25	1st	4	9.0=82%

Placement

F = 95%
C = 91%
D = 84%
E = 84%
G = 82%
A = 77%
B = 73%

Figure 13

Relative Comparison Of Profit and Loss For Each Company

Company	Materials Cost at $25/Inch	$ Sold at $100/Item	Profit/Loss	Placement Based On $ Generated
A	$6,600.00	$2,500.00	-$4,100.00	7th
B	$4,400.00	$2,000.00	-$2,400.00	6th
C	$1,000.00	$3,000.00	-$2,000.00	2nd
D	$1,950.00	$3,000.00	-$1,050.00	3rd
E	$2,750.00	$2,500.00	+$ 250.00	5th
F	$1,400.00	$5,000.00	+$3,600.00	1st
G	$ 625.00	$1,000.00	+ 375.00	4th

Figure 14

These directions include a description of how the management team will be evaluated. (See Figure 15.) All ten of their objectives were created and set up by the instructor. While the categories were selected by the instructor, students set the target goals of keeping the Cost of Goods Manufactured (COGM) for raw materials between 10 to 20 percent and the net profit of $2,500 per production run.

Students also decided to practice on the first seven production runs, then "let it ride" on the eighth and last production run. They decided that they would like to be evaluated based strictly on how they performed on the last production run. If they met all the ten criteria, it was agreed that they would receive an A for this part of their grade.

They were judged on three considerations. The management team would have to meet the ten objectives in order to meet the customer's requirements. They also had to be evaluated by their employees, who were recruited from another class, and the CEO would judge each manager's performance and vice versa. (Incidentally a performance evaluation form is included in the production forms section of the students study guide.) The students decided that 70 percent of their grade would come from the results of the game, 10 percent would be the employees' evaluation, and the remaining 20 percent would be the managers' evaluation of each other. At the last production run, they met the requirements for nine out of ten categories. (Their raw materials ended up being 25 percent, but they made $6,600 profit on the last run.) This profit was primarily due to successful production of a product they designed (a barrel design seen in the Product Spec's section of this manual). The price, delivery and other characteristic for the product were negotiated with the customer.

In conclusion, this last section of the manual also contains a group of multiple choice test questions that can be used to test the students' knowledge. These questions are based on the information contained in the students' Study Guide. Each instructor may wish to supplement these questions with ones discussed in the analysis section of the simulation.

It should be emphasized that while objective questions can be used to test students' knowledge, in my opinion it is more valuable to have the students simply try to produce the best product they can, in the most economic manner possible. When the team runs the game well, they have learned their lessons

well.Because of this I use very few objective questions concerning the game (although I use a few).

Instead, I choose to let the results of the students' performance be the means of their evaluation.

INSTRUCTIONS FOR
THE PRODUCTION GAME, BASIC OPTION

1.   One class period is devoted to developing a management organization,
        review of equipment and study rules of game and product to be produced.

2.   Production day. Product specifications are given to each group of 10
        to 15 student management teams. In a tiered classroom each row can be
        a separate group. Students have 30 minutes to finish as many quality
        products as they can. Shipments are in batches of five items.

3.   Each shipment will be delivered to the customer (3 volunteer students)
        who inspect the shipment to make sure the product meets specifications.
        These specifications include making sure all measurements are within
        1/16", correct color, properly assembled and so forth. If any one item
        in a lot fails inspection, the item is rejected (marked in red) and the
        entire lot is returned to the manufacturing company. The rejected items
        must be kept by the company and counted as scrap at the end of the
        production run. If a lot is rejected, the company cannot resubmit a lot
        for inspection until 2 minutes have passed. If time runs out before any
        lot is fully inspected, the entire lot must be rejected and counted as
        scrap.

GRADING AND SCORING

4.   Each student is a member of a work group based on the row she or he sits
        in. This "company" will produce a product four times during the term
        of the course. Points will be given to each member who is present during
        the production run. The exact amount of the points will be based on
        where the company finishes. For example, a company finishing first will
        receive more points than one which finishes second and so forth. Each
        successive production run is worth more points (see grading attachment).

5.   Students can also receive points based on their CEO's evaluation of their
        efforts during the course. The instructions for the production game
        describe the relationship between the CEO, other management members and
        their employees. The subjectivity or criteria by which the CEO evaluates
        the contribution of others on the team and vice versa can be established
        between the CEO student managers and student workers. The maximum number
        of points that can be acquired here is seen in the grading attachment.
        Think carefully about this area since it is important to reward those
        that contribute the most and not reward the ones that do not contribute.

6.   Students not participating as team members of a production group can act
        as observers of the activity or part of the teacher's assistants. These
        students will be used as inspectors for incoming shipments because the
        customer (teacher) needs to make sure he or she is receiving good
        materials. Those students who act as Quality Control Manager and
        inspectors are responsible not only for managing inspectors and
        controlling materials, but also for recording who used what materials
        and the number of quality products produced, etc. Maximum points for
        these inspectors' efforts are determined by the teacher.

7.   Students, as in any class, are judged on their initiative and participation.   These points are subjective and determined entirely by the teacher.   These points are given at the end of the course.   These points could affect one if, for example, a student were a few points away for a higher grade.   Note that normally, if a student is one point away from a higher grade and has no outstanding "extra credit" effort, he or she <u>will not</u> receive the higher grade.   The only time a student is given the "benefit of the doubt" is when a student has gone above and beyond the call of duty, so to speak.   Activities included here would be:

(1)   frequent classroom participation and discussion

(2)   taking on additional responsibilities

(3)   exceptional efforts and determination in improving grades and performance

Game Grading Attachment

1st Production Run: Points are based strictly on how much <u>good product</u> a
    company produces and which group or companies finished first to last.
    The "companies'" amount of raw materials, work-in-process (WIP) and
    unsold finished materials will be recorded (for comparison's sake, but
    no points will be assigned).

2nd Production Run: Points are based on both production (total numbers
    produced) and amount of square inches of raw materials, work-in-process
    (WIP) and unsold finished materials. Production is not the only factor
    in business success. Controlling overhead is extremely important (70 to
    80% of manufacturing cost is due to materials and inventory). Therefore,
    points are also given for the lowest amount of these materials, WIP and
    finished goods left at the end of the production run. The company with
    the least number of square inches of this inventory will finish first and
    so forth. As in the first run, the square inches of scrap, rework or
    defective product is also recorded (for comparison's sake) but no points
    will be assigned for this category.

3rd Production Run: Points are based on the amount of production, square
    inches of raw material, WIP and finished goods. Inventory is not the
    only material cost, therefore points will also be given for the least
    amount of square inches of scrap, rework or other defective product. The
    other big overhead cost is labor, therefore the percentage of labor
    utilization will also be recorded for all "blue collar" employees. Those
    companies with the highest labor utilization will be noted but no points
    assigned for this category until the last production run.

4th Production Run: The last production run judges each student work group
    based on the four criteria previously discussed. This includes absolute
    production based on number of units produced, square inches of inventory,
    square inches of defective or reworked product, and labor utilization.

    *NOTE: If any student work group, except for first place finishers,
                  fails to achieve some improvement in performance, a two point
                  (per production run per student) deduction will be made to
                  the entire work group.

    *NOTE: Near the end of the course the Japanese Production Company
                  (JPC) will enter the market. Their production numbers,
                  square inches of inventory and defective product, as well as
                  labor utilization, will be the benchmark for the whole class.
                  Any company able to meet or beat these numbers will receive
                  extra credit points.

The breakdown of these points is seen on the following pages.

SUMMARY OF PRODUCTION GAME POINTS

(1)   Maximum points to produce good products   45 points
(2)   Beating JPG benchmark   5 points
(3)   CEO's evaluation student's work effort in   <u>10 points</u>
      their group (CEO receives the average score
      from all work team, after high and low score
      has been thrown out)

                    Total points   *60 points

*Together these points for the production game account for slightly over
10% of your total grade.

```
Test 1   . . . . . . . . . . . . . . . . . .  100 pts.
Test 2   . . . . . . . . . . . . . . . . . .  100 pts.
Test 3   . . . . . . . . . . . . . . . . . .  100 pts.
Test 4   . . . . . . . . . . . . . . . . . .  100 pts.
Quizzes . . . . . . . . . . . . . . . . . . . 40 pts.
Production Game . . . . . . . . . . . . . . . 60 pts.
Possible Bonus Points . . . . . . . . . . . 0-10 pts.
(Given for innovations and work above
and beyond the call of duty)
```

Extra credit might be given for such things as developing new forms or other
activities that improved ability to manage the production company, exceptional
classroom participation and for doing an outstanding job as CEO, etc.

EXAMPLE OF DIRECTIONS
FOR
THE PRODUCTION GAME, ADVANCED OPTION

Noble Manufacturing Company produces a variety of products. They act as a job shop for House of Brokerage, Inc. Positions for Noble are to be filled by you and other group members.

You, as your Study Guide notes, may want to establish finance, quality control, production, inventory and purchasing responsibilities, but your company's organization is entirely up to you. Regardless of responsibilities, make sure your organization is able to meet emergencies and changing production requirements based upon changing markets.

As Noble personnel you are primarily concerned with productivity, quality, and profit. This is most easily accomplished by focusing on cycle time, which is the time from the moment the customer's order is accepted until the product is delivered to the customer. In order to add a perspective to production your company has an initial capital, as well as some production equipment and inventory. Raw materials can be purchased from Muscleman Construction Works and finished goods can be sold to the House of Brokerage, Inc. The Brokerage company will notify you of market conditions at the time your plant begins operation. Market conditions and needs for a variety of products may change, but you will be notified of those changes by your Brokerage company.

Products of Noble Manufacturing Company consist of items assembled and manufactured from one-half sheets of construction paper. Your organization will be notified by the House of Brokerage of product specifications and needs at the time your plant begins operations and as market needs change.

Raw materials are sheets of construction paper. Finished goods consist of paper products that must conform to standards outlined on the Product Specification Sheet. You will need to work out some way of making sure that product specifications are met, since quality is an important issue of House of Brokerage. You will also need to make sure the following data is gathered:

*Total output (volume).
*Labor utilization (total minutes worked and percent for each time each
   employee was actually working).
*Maintaining proper product mix (i.e., meeting market demand).
*Estimating dollars Noble has in terms of raw materials, in-process and
   finished goods at the end of your production cycle.
*Other relevant measures, as needed.

Records should be set up and kept up to date. In determining volume and product mix (#3) you

can only count finished goods in inventory at the end of any production period. Goods in-process are not to

be counted, so you will need a place to store your finished goods inventory.

You may purchase additional raw materials from your supplier (Muscleman), but you should

allow three minutes lead time before you can receive raw materials. Out of stock material can only be filled

after ten minutes.

Raw materials can be purchased from Muscleman at a cost of $800 per sheet (except for yellow

sheets which cost $900). Every transport of finished goods to the Brokerage Company will cost $200, with

a maximum cargo of 20 items per transport. You may pay each employee a salary which is decided by

management at the end of each production cycle (example, seven dollars per minute worked or "on the

clock").

Starting income is $50,000 as well as some initial raw materials and production equipment. Each

product produced by your organization must meet rigid quality standards. Dimensions of products are to be

within 1/16 of an inch (unless otherwise noted). Each product must also meet stress tests (not fall apart

under normal usage). It is up to the Brokerage Company to decide finished goods inspection (at their

location). If products fail to meet specifications, products will be returned to Noble at their expense. If a sample is rejected, that product is rejected and becomes useless. All other items in the lot are returned to the manufacturing company for 100 percent inspection.

You will not need a sales force but you will need someone to get market and product requirements. In meeting changes in market requirements excess, finished goods and raw materials may be carrried over to the next period, but there is a holding cost for each. Holding cost for finished inventory is $25 per item that is held at the start of the next production period. Raw materials costs due before start of production period are $25 per square inch of material (round dollars to nearest $50). Work-in-process at the end of a production period cannot be counted as finished inventory and thus becomes scrap. Scrap cannot be used in the production process.

You should try to produce as large a volume as possible of quality products to meet market demands. It is important to meet delivery dates. There is a 10 percent late charge (based on total value of lot) if the job is not delivered on time. There is a 20 percent charge for deliveries over two minutes and a 30 percent cost for those that are three to five minutes late. No delivery over five minutes late will be accepted. If late deliveries continue to be a problem, greater cost will be incurred at each production run. Try to maximize both the productivity and creativity of those that do work for Noble. It is recommended that you maintain as much flexibility as possible to deal with changing production and marketing requirements. Although self direction is recommended, try to provide assistance and help for personnel who are having problems, and try to get all personnel involved in the production process.

Grading for the simulation will be based on meeting the customers' expectations. A sample of those expectations is seen in Figure 15.

GRADING FOR THE ADVANCED OPTION

CUSTOMER EXPECTATIONS

The following are ten different items that we should strive for to maintain good customer relations and a competitive edge. (Also, these items are what 70 percent of our company simulation grades will be based on; therefore, we need to achieve them if we want full credit).

<u>GOAL</u> <u>OBJECTIVE</u>

Quantity

    1. Correct lot size.
    2. On-time delivery.
       <u>Availability</u> is part of a reasonable customer
       expectation.

Quality

    3. Adherence to all dimensions.
    4. Correct combination of colors.
    5. Sturdy construction (shake test).
    6. Attractive appearance (sharp lettering, crisp lines, no
       smudges or marks on material).

Productivity

    7. 85 percent labor utilization rate.
    8. Scrap cost at 10 percent of COGM.
    9. Raw material between 10 percent and 20 percent of
       COGM.
       <u>Cost efficiency</u>--without this we will not be in
       business, and our customers will not have a supplier,
       or if we do stay in business, our customers won't get
       products made at a reasonable price.

Profits

    10. Net profit margin of 10 percent and $2,500 profit
       per production run.
       <u>Dependability</u>--without reasonable profits we can't
       stay in business, and if we bust, our customers lose a
       supplier. Reliability is critical when companies choose
       suppliers.

Figure 15

MULTIPLE CHOICE TEST QUESTIONS

1. The <u>Group Clock In/Out</u> report is used to:
    a. record the time when <u>an</u> employee begins or ends   _____c
        his or her work shift.
    b. record the start/stop times associated with part-
        time employees.
    c. measure and record the total production time of all
        of your employees.
    d. measure the time equipment used.

2. The <u>Labor Utilization</u> Figures report is used to:
    a. record the start/stop times associated with part-   _____c
        time employees.
    b. record the time <u>an</u> employee begins or ends his or her
        work shift.
    c. measure and record the total production time of
        all of your employees.
    d. measure the time equipment is used.

3. The <u>Quality/Productivity</u> report records:
    a. record the time when <u>an</u> employee begins or ends   _____d
        his or her work shift.
    b. record the start/stop times associated with part-
        time employees.
    c. measure and record the total production time of
        all of your employees.
    d. measure the time equipment is used.

4. WIP stands for:
    a. work in process.
    b. worker involvement programs.   _____a
    c. work in progress.
    d. none of the above.

5. Which of the statements is true?
    a. There is one best way to organize a company.
    b. Assess your design of your organization before   _____b
        examining how you executed your plan.
    c. The Board of Directors has ultimate responsibility
        for running companies in the Production Game.
    d. An asterisk (*) refers to the basic option of the
        game.

6. "If you can't measure it, you can't manage it" refers to
    the fact that:
    a. a manager should depend on time and motion experts   _____b
        to measure employee efficiency.
    b. to improve your performance you will have to know
        where you stand and where you want to be.
    c. you can't really manage jobs that don't have a
        service basis.
    d. if you don't know how good something is, you don't
        know how to control it.

7. The <u>individual time card</u> is used to:
    a. measure and record the total production time of all   _____c
        of your employees.
    b. measure the time equipment is used.
    c. record the time when an employee or other personnel begins
        and ends his or her work shifts.
    d. record the start/stop times associated with part-
        time employees.

8. Small lots
    a. reduce the amount of inventory a company has.   _____d
    b. make the flow of work smoother.
    c. reduce slack time.
    d. all of the above.

9. The ideal lot size is
    a. zero.   _____b
    b. one.
    c. ten.
    d. one hundred.

10. JIT
    a. reduces WIP.   _____d
    b. demands a flexible work force.
    c. improves quality.
    d. all of the above.
    e. none of the above.

11. It is usually wise for management to try to:
    a. have 100 percent labor utilization.   _____e
    b. JIC.
    c. order all inventory through EOQ's.
    d. all of the above.
    e. none of the above.

12. Making a die improves:
    a. labor utilization.   _____c
    b. inventory.
    c. quality.
    d. all the above.

13. A go/no go gage:
    a. is a poor quality alternative.   ____b
    b. reduces the skill needed to inspect products.
    c. is used in inventory control.
    d. is an instrument that tells you if something is
       working properly.

14. According to your simulation study guide, in <u>quality</u>
    today:
    a. customers do not want to inspect incoming shipments.   ____a
    b. the trend is to increase inspection of incoming
       materials.
    c. the trend is to decrease in-process inspection and focus on
       designing quality in.
    d. the trend is to mainly rely on end of the line inspection.

15. According to your simulation study guide, in inventory
    today:
    a. everyone is trying to reduce lot sizes.   ____a
    b. everyone is trying to increase lot sizes.
    c. the trend is to order materials by EOQ's.
    d. inventory is not as much a problem for companies as quality is.

16. In the production game assessing quality consists of:
    a. measuring measurements.   ____d
    b. focusing on general appearance.
    c. evaluating stress tests.
    d. all of the above.
    e. none of the above.

17. The best way to improve quality is to:
    a. do frequent inspections.   ____b
    b. design quality in.
    c. get employee involvement.
    d. fix problems immediately.

18. The best place to resolve quality problems is:
    a. in management meetings.   ____c
    b. before delivery to customers.
    c. on the assembly line.
    d. with negotiation with your competitors.

19. If every piece and every subassembly of a product is
    within specifications, then
    a. you can be assured that the product will be a good ____b
       one.
    b. you can still produce a product that doesn't meet
       your customer's requirements.
    c. most of the time the product will still be out of
       spec.
    d. you know something is wrong.

20. The best advice as far as customer relations are concerned is:
    a. see no evil, hear no evil.   _____d
    b. limit your assumptions.
    c. too much customer feedback can be a risk.
    d. none of the above.

21. As far as negotiation goes, the study guide recommends:
    a. it's wise to have the CEO do the negotiation since   _____d
       he or she can eliminate delays.
    b. negotiate an increase in price for better service
       <u>after</u> management has already sealed the deal with
       the customer.
    c. have customers initial <u>all</u> changes.
    d. all of the above.

22. The simulation study guide notes that the single most
    common suggestion made by practicing CEO's, plant managers
    and others is to:
    a. get to know the customer.   _____b
    b. do a first-piece check.
    c. control inventory cost.
    d. make products producible and profitable.

23. Double checking each step of the assembly process for
    quality problems is called:
    a. die setting.   _____c
    b. JIT.
    c. first-piece check.
    d. flow charting.

24. According to the information in the production booklet,
    quality can be improved through
    a. making a die.   _____d
    b. a first-piece check.
    c. use of a template.
    d. all of the above.

25. The tools used to identify both the number of job steps and the time
    each step takes are: (2 answers)
    a. flow charts.   _____a&d
    b. first-piece checks.
    c. JIT.
    d. templates.

26. JIT improves:
    a. inventory size.   _____d
    b. product quality.
    c. productivity.
    d. all of the above.
    e. none of the above.

27.   Short cycle times occur when companies:
      a.   do it right the first time.   _____a
      b.   use multiple vendors.
      c.   produce in large lot sizes.
      d.   provide extensive employee training.

28.   According to the simulation, effectively designing an
      organization is critical to success; this includes:
      a.   identifying each person's responsibilities.   _____d
      b.   deciding whether you need to be a job shop or
           repetitive arrangement.
      c.   determining the division of work.
      d.   all of the above.
      e.   none of the above.

29.   The most common mistake made during a production run is:
      a.   keeping too high of an inventory.   _____b
      b.   the CEO and other managers getting directly involved
           in producing a product.
      c.   producing poor quality products.
      d.   not meeting customer expectations.

30.   Which of the following statements is true?
      a.   Union shops are in favor of cross training.   _____e
      b.   CEO and other managers should become directly
           involved in helping produce products in time of
           crisis.
      c.   Have your staff and engineers first analyze problems
           and develop solutions before having to get production
           personnel involved in the decision.
      d.   all of the above.
      e.   none of the above.

31.   According to the Production Game, the objective World Class
      competitors:
      a.   make 100% good product.   _____d
      b.   have zero inventory.
      c.   have no or little WIP.
      d.   all of the above.
      e.   none of the above.

32.   The <u>Square Inch Measuring Board</u> can be used to measure
      a.   scrap.   _____d
      b.   WIP.
      c.   raw materials.
      d.   all of the above.

33. The simulation exercise notes that the ultimate production
    objective is:
    a. waste not want not.   _____b
    b. do it right the first time.
    c. if you can measure it, you can't improve it.
    d. zero inventory.
    e. none of the above.

34. The Production Game booklet notes that you can increase
    the percentage of time that you are utilizing production
    equipment using:
    a. flextime.   _____d
    b. multi-skills.
    c. better scheduling.
    d. all of the above.
    e. none of the above.

35. Which of the following statements is true?
    a. Management has done their job when they find out   _____c
        what the customer does not want in the way of
        products or services.
    b. If the product specifications are not on the product
        sheet, then management is not responsible or accountable
        for them.
    c. Prototypes are best for complex products.
    d. The only drawback to a prototype is that it forces the
        production process to start later.

36. The simulation booklet emphasizes that the single most
    important management tool for a company to use in order to
    become more productive is:
    a. to control inventory.   _____b
    b. its people.
    c. to reduce cost.
    d. to improve its quality.

37. It is management's responsibility to:
    a. find out what the customer wants.   _____d
    b. find out what the customer does not want.
    c. neither a nor b.
    d. both a and b.

38. Which of the following is true?
    a. If the product specifications are not on the product   _____c
        sheet, it is not management's problem.
    b. It is unwise for your designers to visit your customer
        since this is best left to those who best understand the
        customer, namely marketing.
    c. During a production run, it is wise to have upper manage-
        ment visit the customer.
    d. none of the above.

39.   Flow charts in the simulation are used to:
    a.   identify the number of job steps.   _____d
    b.   determine the time each job step takes.
    c.   find the critical path.
    d.   all of the above.

40.   Who should use the product spec sheets?
    a.   Manufacturing.   _____d
    b.   Quality Control.
    c.   Human Resources.
    d.   all of the above.

41.   As noted in the simulation exercise, JIT requires
    a.   cross training.   _____d
    b.   a flexible work force.
    c.   a nontraditional approach to inventory control.
    d.   all of the above.
    e.   none of the above.

42.   The study guide notes that in order to implement JIT it is
    recommended that you encourage:
    a.   cross training.   _____a
    b.   clear, distinct job classifications.
    c.   narrow job descriptions.
    d.   skills testing.

43.   Before a production run, the study guide emphasizes that the
    type of training for the job should include:
    a.   training in safety requirements.   _____d
    b.   training in production standards.
    c.   input from production employees.
    d.   all of the above.

44.   One of the statements is false; which one is it?
    a.   When problems occur, fix them immediately.   _____c
    b.   First-piece checks are ways of improving quality.
    c.   JIT is a push system.
    d.   Process planners are liaisons between design and
        manufacturing.

45.   A liaison like a process planner:
    a.   is for improving communication between design and   _____a
        manufacturing.
    b.   determines which process will be used to manufacture
        an item.
    c.   uses a set of rules to go by that determines which
        process will be used.
    d.   is the same as a design engineer.

46. A flow chart helps managers determine:
    a. how long each production step takes.   _____d
    b. the number of production steps.
    c. how many people are needed at work stations.
    d. all of the above.

47. From a design standpoint:
    a. it's impossible to have too much input from the   _____e
       management team.
    b. it's always wise to choose the easier designs.
    c. focus on profitability and producibility will take
       care of itself.
    d. all of the above.
    e. none of the above.

INDEX

EXAMPLE OF

STENCIL SHEETS

STOP

STOP   STOP   STOP

STOP   STOP   STOP

STOP   STOP   STOP

STOP   STOP   STOP

STOP   STOP   STOP

STOP   STOP   STOP

STOP   STOP   STOP

STOP

STOP

STOP STOP STOP

STOP STOP STOP

STOP STOP STOP

STOP STOP STOP

STOP STOP STOP

STOP STOP STOP

STOP STOP STOP

STOP

STOP   STOP   STOP

STOP   STOP   STOP

STOP   STOP   STOP

STOP   STOP   STOP

STOP   STOP   STOP

STOP   STOP   STOP

STOP   STOP   STOP

STOP

STOP STOP STOP

STOP STOP STOP

STOP STOP STOP

STOP STOP STOP

STOP STOP STOP

STOP STOP STOP

STOP STOP STOP

YIELD

YIELD

YIELD

YIELD

YIELD

YIELD

YIELD

YIELD

YIELD

YIELD

YIELD

YIELD

YIELD

YIELD

YIELD

YIELD

YIELD

YIELD

YIELD

YIELD

YIELD

YIELD

YIELD

YIELD

YIELD

YIELD

YIELD

YIELD

YIELD

YIELD

YIELD

YIELD

YIELD

YIELD

YIELD

YIELD

YIELD

YIELD

YIELD

YIELD

YIELD

YIELD

YIELD

YIELD

YIELD

YIELD

YIELD

YIELD

YIELD

YIELD

YIELD

YIELD

YIELD

YIELD

YIELD

YIELD

YIELD

YIELD

YIELD

YIELD

YIELD

YIELD

YIELD

YIELD YIELD

A-13

YIELD

YIELD

YIELD

YIELD

YIELD

YIELD

YIELD

YIELD

YIELD

YIELD

YIELD

YIELD

YIELD

YIELD

YIELD

YIELD

YIELD

YIELD

YIELD

YIELD

YIELD

YIELD

YIELD

YIELD

YIELD

YIELD

YIELD

YIELD

YIELD

YIELD

YIELD

YIELD

YIELD

YIELD

YIELD

YIELD

YIELD

YIELD

YIELD

YIELD

YIELD

YIELD

YIELD

YIELD

YIELD

YIELD

YIELD

YIELD

YIELD

YIELD

YIELD

YIELD

YIELD

YIELD

YIELD

YIELD

YIELD

YIELD

YIELD

YIELD

YIELD

YIELD

YIELD

YIELD

YIELD

YIELD

YIELD

YIELD

YIELD

YIELD

YIELD

YIELD

YIELD

YIELD

YIELD

YIELD

YIELD

YIELD

YIELD

YIELD

YIELD

YIELD

YIELD

YIELD

YIELD

YIELD

YIELD

YIELD

YIELD

YIELD

YIELD

YIELD

YIELD

YIELD

YIELD

YIELD

YIELD

YIELD

YIELD

YIELD

YIELD

YIELD

YIELD

YIELD

YIELD

YIELD

YIELD

YIELD

YIELD

YIELD

YIELD

YIELD

YIELD

YIELD

YIELD

YIELD

YIELD

YIELD

YIELD

YIELD

YIELD

YIELD

YIELD

YIELD

YIELD

NOTICE **NOTICE**

NOTICE **NOTICE**

NOTICE **NOTICE**

NOTICE **NOTICE**

NOTICE **NOTICE**

NOTICE **NOTICE**

NOTICE **NOTICE**

NOTICE **NOTICE**

NOTICE **NOTICE**

NOTICE **NOTICE**

NOTICE **NOTICE**

NOTICE **NOTICE**

NOTICE   **NOTICE**

NOTICE   **NOTICE**

NOTICE   **NOTICE**

NOTICE   **NOTICE**

NOTICE   **NOTICE**

NOTICE   **NOTICE**

NOTICE   **NOTICE**

NOTICE   **NOTICE**

NOTICE   **NOTICE**

NOTICE   **NOTICE**

NOTICE   **NOTICE**

NOTICE   **NOTICE**

NOTICE **NOTICE**

NOTICE **NOTICE**

NOTICE **NOTICE**

NOTICE **NOTICE**

NOTICE **NOTICE**

NOTICE **NOTICE**

NOTICE **NOTICE**

NOTICE **NOTICE**

NOTICE **NOTICE**

NOTICE **NOTICE**

NOTICE **NOTICE**

NOTICE **NOTICE**

NOTICE **NOTICE**

A-25

NOTICE NOTICE
NOTICE NOTICE
NOTICE NOTICE
NOTICE NOTICE
NOTICE NOTICE
NOTICE NOTICE
NOTICE NOTICE
NOTICE NOTICE
NOTICE NOTICE
NOTICE NOTICE
NOTICE NOTICE
NOTICE NOTICE
NOTICE NOTICE

BE CAREFUL	BE CAREFUL	BE CAREFUL
BE CAREFUL	BE CAREFUL	BE CAREFUL
BE CAREFUL	BE CAREFUL	BE CAREFUL
BE CAREFUL	BE CAREFUL	BE CAREFUL
BE CAREFUL	BE CAREFUL	BE CAREFUL
BE CAREFUL	BE CAREFUL	BE CAREFUL
BE CAREFUL	BE CAREFUL	BE CAREFUL
BE CAREFUL	BE CAREFUL	BE CAREFUL
BE CAREFUL	BE CAREFUL	BE CAREFUL
BE CAREFUL	BE CAREFUL	BE CAREFUL

BE CAREFUL	BE CAREFUL	BE CAREFUL
BE CAREFUL	BE CAREFUL	BE CAREFUL
BE CAREFUL	BE CAREFUL	BE CAREFUL
BE CAREFUL	BE CAREFUL	BE CAREFUL
BE CAREFUL	BE CAREFUL	BE CAREFUL
BE CAREFUL	BE CAREFUL	BE CAREFUL
BE CAREFUL	BE CAREFUL	BE CAREFUL
BE CAREFUL	BE CAREFUL	BE CAREFUL
BE CAREFUL	BE CAREFUL	BE CAREFUL
BE CAREFUL	BE CAREFUL	BE CAREFUL

BE CAREFUL	BE CAREFUL	BE CAREFUL
BE CAREFUL	BE CAREFUL	BE CAREFUL
BE CAREFUL	BE CAREFUL	BE CAREFUL
BE CAREFUL	BE CAREFUL	BE CAREFUL
BE CAREFUL	BE CAREFUL	BE CAREFUL
BE CAREFUL	BE CAREFUL	BE CAREFUL
BE CAREFUL	BE CAREFUL	BE CAREFUL
BE CAREFUL	BE CAREFUL	BE CAREFUL
BE CAREFUL	BE CAREFUL	BE CAREFUL
BE CAREFUL	BE CAREFUL	BE CAREFUL

BE CAREFUL	**BE CAREFUL**	**BE CAREFUL**
BE CAREFUL	**BE CAREFUL**	**BE CAREFUL**
BE CAREFUL	**BE CAREFUL**	**BE CAREFUL**
BE CAREFUL	**BE CAREFUL**	**BE CAREFUL**
BE CAREFUL	**BE CAREFUL**	**BE CAREFUL**
BE CAREFUL	**BE CAREFUL**	**BE CAREFUL**
BE CAREFUL	**BE CAREFUL**	**BE CAREFUL**
BE CAREFUL	**BE CAREFUL**	**BE CAREFUL**
BE CAREFUL	**BE CAREFUL**	**BE CAREFUL**
BE CAREFUL	**BE CAREFUL**	**BE CAREFUL**

DANGER	DANGER	DANGER
DANGER	DANGER	DANGER
DANGER	DANGER	DANGER
DANGER	DANGER	DANGER
DANGER	DANGER	DANGER
DANGER	DANGER	DANGER
DANGER	DANGER	DANGER
DANGER	DANGER	DANGER
DANGER	DANGER	DANGER
DANGER	DANGER	DANGER
DANGER	DANGER	DANGER
DANGER	DANGER	DANGER

DANGER DANGER DANGER

DANGER DANGER DANGER

DANGER DANGER DANGER

DANGER DANGER DANGER

DANGER DANGER DANGER

DANGER DANGER DANGER

DANGER DANGER DANGER

DANGER DANGER DANGER

DANGER DANGER DANGER

DANGER DANGER DANGER

DANGER DANGER DANGER

DANGER DANGER DANGER

DANGER DANGER DANGER

DANGER DANGER DANGER

DANGER DANGER DANGER

DANGER DANGER DANGER

DANGER DANGER DANGER

DANGER DANGER DANGER

DANGER DANGER DANGER

DANGER DANGER DANGER

DANGER DANGER DANGER

DANGER DANGER DANGER

DANGER DANGER DANGER

DANGER DANGER DANGER

A-41

DANGER DANGER DANGER
DANGER DANGER DANGER
DANGER DANGER DANGER
DANGER DANGER DANGER
DANGER DANGER DANGER
DANGER DANGER DANGER
DANGER DANGER DANGER
DANGER DANGER DANGER
DANGER DANGER DANGER
DANGER DANGER DANGER
DANGER DANGER DANGER
DANGER DANGER DANGER

EXAMPLE OF

MONEY USED IN THE SIMULATION

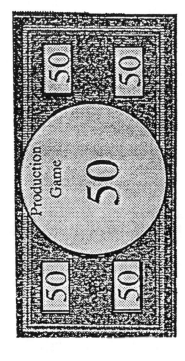 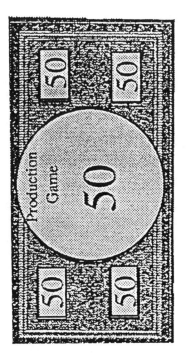 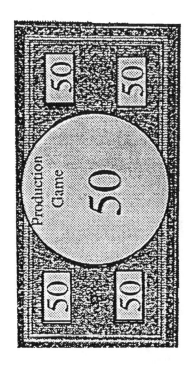

 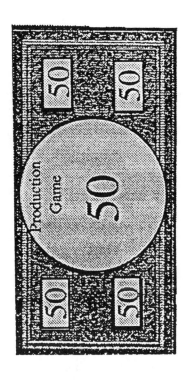 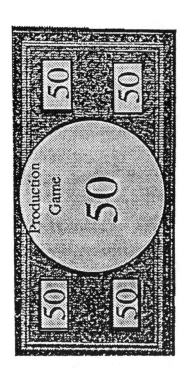

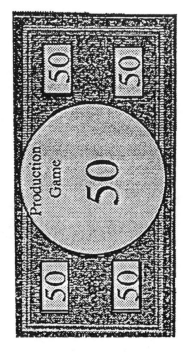
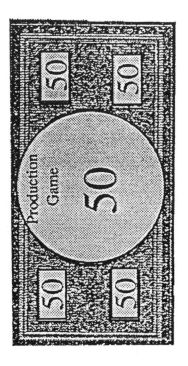
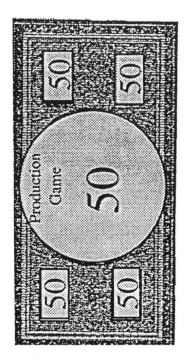

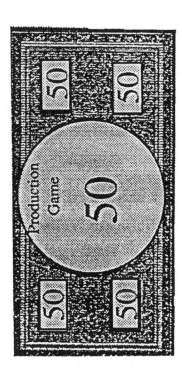
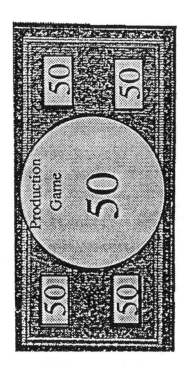

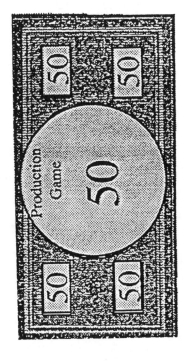
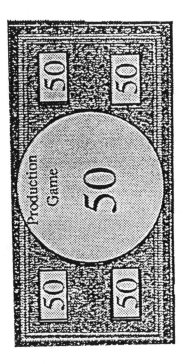
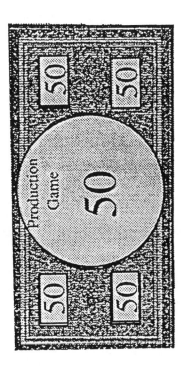

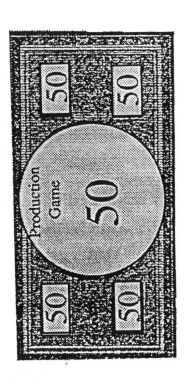
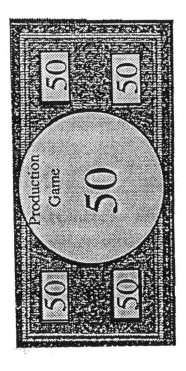

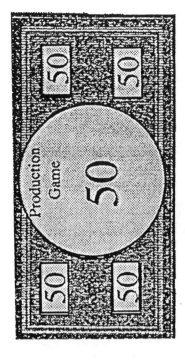 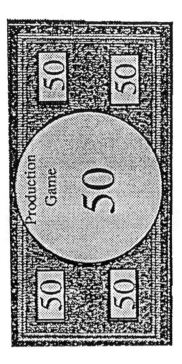 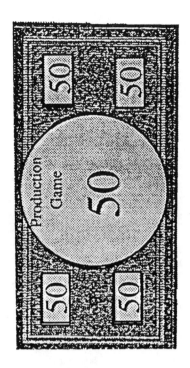

 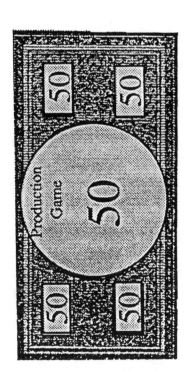 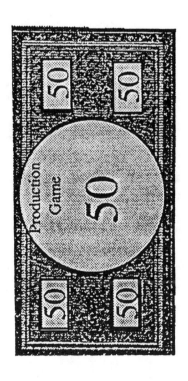

B-11

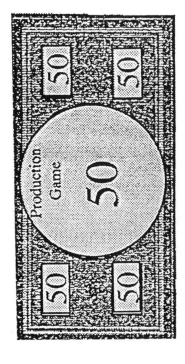
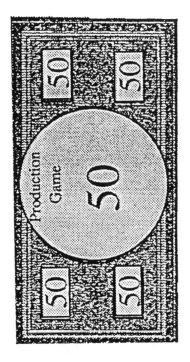
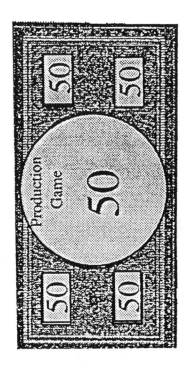

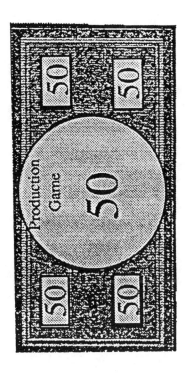
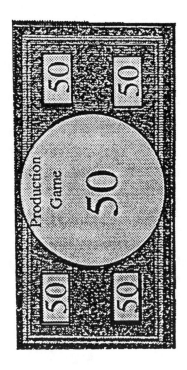

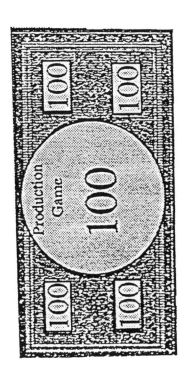

B-15

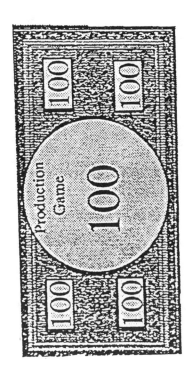

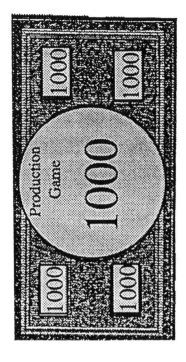

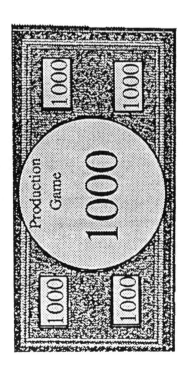

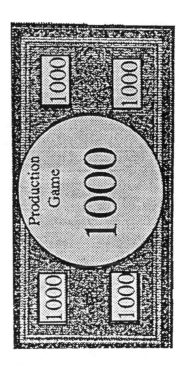

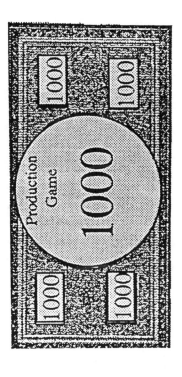